MW01596237

OFFICE TREATMENT OF SCHIZOPHRENIA

Clinical Practice
Number 11

Judith H. Gold, M.D., F.R.C.P.(C)
Series Editor

OFFICE TREATMENT OF SCHIZOPHRENIA

Edited by

MARY V. SEEMAN, M.D., F.R.C.P.(C)

Psychiatrist-in-Chief, Mount Sinai Hospital, Toronto, Ontario;
Professor of Psychiatry, University of Toronto

STANLEY E. GREBEN, M.D., F.R.C.P.(C)

Consultant, Mount Sinai Hospital, Toronto, Ontario; Professor
of Psychiatry and Professor of Psychotherapy, University of
Toronto

1400 K Street, N.W.
Washington, DC 20005

Note: The authors have worked to ensure that all information in this book concerning drug dosages, schedules, and routes of administration is accurate as of the time of publication and consistent with standards set by the U.S. Food and Drug Administration and the general medical community. As medical research and practice advance, however, therapeutic standards may change. For this reason and because human and mechanical errors sometimes occur, we recommend that readers follow the advice of a physician who is directly involved in their care or the care of a member of their family.

Copyright © 1990 American Psychiatric Press, Inc.
ALL RIGHTS RESERVED
Manufactured in the United States of America
First Edition

93   92   91   90   4   3   2

The paper used in this publication meets the minimum requirements of the American National Standard for Information Sciences—Permanence of Paper for Printed Library Materials, ANSI Z39.48-1984.   ∞

Library of Congress Cataloging-in-Publication Data

Office treatment of schizophrenia/edited by Mary V. Seeman, Stanley E. Greben—1st ed.
      p.   cm.—(Clinical practice: no. 11)
      Includes bibliographical references.
      ISBN 0-88048-191-9 (alk. paper)
      1. Schizophrenia—Treatment.   I. Seeman, M. V. (Mary Violette), 1935–   . II. Greben, Stanley E. III. Series.
      [DNLM: 1. Schizophrenia—therapy. W1 CL767J no. 11/WM 203 032]
RC514.034   1989
616.89′82—dc20
DNLM/DLC   89–17559
for Library of Congress   CIP

Contents

CONTRIBUTORS vii

INTRODUCTION TO THE CLINICAL PRACTICE
SERIES ix

INTRODUCTION xiii

1 Long-Term Nature of Treatment 1
Stanley E. Greben, M.D., F.R.C.P.(C)

2 Assessment 19
Mary V. Seeman, M.D., F.R.C.P.(C)

3 Engaging Patient and Family in Treatment 39
Mary V. Seeman, M.D., F.R.C.P.(C)

4 Individual Psychotherapy 59
Stanley E. Greben, M.D., F.R.C.P.(C)

5 Family Therapy 79
Leopoldo Chagoya, M.D., F.R.C.P.(C)

6 Group Therapy 99
Paul Goldhamer, M.D., F.R.C.P.(C)
Molyn Leszcz, M.D., F.R.C.P.(C)

7 Antipsychotic Pharmacotherapy 123
Mary V. Seeman, M.D., F.R.C.P.(C)

8 Adjunct Therapies 141
Peter Brown, M.D., F.R.C.P.(C)

9 Networking   *161*
   Paul Goldhamer, M.D., F.R.C.P.(C)

10 Dealing With Crisis   *177*
   Rodney O. N. Slonim, M.D., F.R.C.P.(C)

11 Conclusion: Essentials and Prospects   *195*
   for the Future
   Stanley E. Greben, M.D., F.R.C.P.(C)

Contributors

Peter Brown, M.D., F.R.C.P.(C)
Head of Consultation-Liaison Service, Head of Research, and Staff Psychiatrist, Department of Psychiatry, Mount Sinai Hospital, Toronto, Ontario; Assistant Professor, Department of Psychiatry, University of Toronto

Leopoldo Chagoya, M.D., F.R.C.P.(C)
Coordinator, Family and Couple Therapy Clinic, and Staff Psychiatrist, Mount Sinai Hospital, Toronto, Ontario; Associate Professor, Department of Psychiatry, University of Toronto

Paul M. Goldhamer, M.D., F.R.C.P.(C)
Coordinator of Schizophrenia Clinic, Staff Psychiatrist, Mount Sinai Hospital, Toronto, Ontario; Assistant Professor, Department of Psychiatry, University of Toronto

Stanley E. Greben, M.D., F.R.C.P.(C)
Consultant, Department of Psychiatry, Mount Sinai Hospital, Toronto, Ontario; Consultant, Clarke Institute of Psychiatry, Toronto, Ontario; Consultant, Department of Psychiatry, Toronto Western Hospital; Senior Consultant, Baycrest Centre for Geriatric Care, Toronto, Ontario; Professor of Psychiatry and Professor of Psychotherapy, University of Toronto

Molyn Leszcz, M.D., F.R.C.P.(C)
Coordinator of Group Psychotherapy, and Staff Psychiatrist, Mount Sinai Hospital, Toronto, Ontario; Coordinator of Group Psychotherapy, Baycrest Centre for Geriatric Care, Toronto, Ontario; Senior Group Psychotherapy Consultant, To-

ronto General Hospital; Assistant Professor, Department of Psychiatry, University of Toronto

Mary V. Seeman, M.D., F.R.C.P.(C)
Psychiatrist-in-Chief, Mount Sinai Hospital, Toronto, Ontario; Consultant, Clarke Institute of Psychiatry, Toronto, Ontario; Consultant, Baycrest Centre for Geriatric Care, Toronto, Ontario; Professor of Psychiatry, University of Toronto

Rodney O. N. Slonim, M.D., F.R.C.P.(C)
Head, Emergency and Crisis Intervention Service, Head, Community Service Clinic, and Staff Psychiatrist, Mount Sinai Hospital, Toronto, Ontario; Assistant Professor, Department of Psychiatry, University of Toronto

Introduction
to the Clinical Practice Series

Over the years of its existence the series of monographs entitled *Clinical Insights* gradually became focused on providing current, factual, and theoretical material of interest to the clinician working outside of a hospital setting. To reflect this orientation, the name of the Series has been changed to *Clinical Practice.*

The Clinical Practice Series will provide readers with books that give the mental health clinician a practical clinical approach to a variety of psychiatric problems. These books will provide up-to-date literature reviews and emphasize the most recent treatment methods. Thus, the publications in the Series will interest clinicians working both in psychiatry and in the other mental health professions.

Each year a number of books will be published dealing with all aspects of clinical practice. In addition, from time to time when appropriate, the publications may be revised and updated. Thus, the Series will provide quick access to relevant and important areas of psychiatric practice. Some books in the Series will be authored by a person considered to be an expert in that particular area; others will be edited by such an expert who will also draw together other knowledgeable authors to produce a comprehensive overview of that topic.

Some of the books in the Clinical Practice Series will have their foundation in presentations at an Annual Meeting of the American Psychiatric Association. All will contain the most recently available information on the subjects discussed. Theoretical and scientific data will be applied to clinical situations, and case illustrations will be utilized in order to make the material even more relevant for the practitioner. Thus, the Clinical Practice Series should provide educational reading in a compact format especially written for the mental health clinician–psychiatrist.

Judith H. Gold, M.D., F.R.C.P.(C)
Series Editor
Clinical Practice Series

Clinical Practice Series Titles

Treating Chronically Mentally Ill Women (#1)
Edited by Leona L. Bachrach, Ph.D., and Carol C. Nadelson, M.D.

Divorce as a Developmental Process (#2)
Edited by Judith H. Gold, M.D., F.R.C.P.(C)

Family Violence: Emerging Issues of a National Crisis (#3)
Edited by Leah J. Dickstein, M.D., and Carol C. Nadelson, M.D.

Anxiety and Depressive Disorders in the Medical Patient (#4)
By Leonard R. Derogatis, Ph.D., and Thomas N. Wise, M.D.

Anxiety: New Findings for the Clinician (#5)
Edited by Peter Roy-Byrne, M.D.

The Neuroleptic Malignant Syndrome and Related Conditions (#6)
By Arthur Lazarus, M.D., Stephan C. Mann, M.D., and Stanley N. Caroff, M.D.

Juvenile Homicide (#7)
Edited by Elissa P. Benedek, M.D., and Dewey G. Cornell, Ph.D.

Measuring Mental Illness: Psychometric Assessment for Clinicians (#8)
Edited by Scott Wetzler, Ph.D.

Family Involvement in Treatment of the Frail Elderly (#9)
Edited by Marion Zucker Goldstein, M.D.

Psychiatric Care of Migrants (#10)
By Joseph J. Westermeyer, M.D.

Office Treatment of Schizophrenia (#11)
Edited by Mary V. Seeman, M.D., F.R.C.P.(C), and Stanley E. Greben, M.D., F.R.C.P.(C)

The Psychosocial Impact of Job Loss (#12)
By Nick Kates, M.B.B.S., Barrie S. Greiff, M.D., and Duane Q. Hagan, M.D.

New Perspectives on Narcissism (#13)
Edited by Eric M. Plakun, M.D.

Introduction

This book is written to help the psychiatrist in office practice with the challenging and sometimes heartbreaking task of treating individuals who suffer with schizophrenia. Many of these patients are young, since schizophrenia strikes at a time in life when the adolescent or young adult is about to embark on his or her life's journey. Dreams of accomplishment and intimacy and contentment are interrupted by this illness, and the psychiatrist is asked to revive the interrupted dreams by making the illness disappear. This task is all the more onerous for a clinician working alone without immediate colleagues with whom to share the concerns, doubts, and hopes that such work arouses.

Our goal is to impart to the clinician in office practice the sense of excitement that can accompany difficult work with difficult problems. The patient with schizophrenia requires attentive care in order to achieve a diminution of symptoms and a relative freedom from those sequelae that are avoidable. He or she also requires sensitivity to personal needs and a long-term commitment to help with a lifetime of taxing illness. The patient must be treated first as a person and only secondarily as a sufferer from a specific disease process. The schizophrenic patient needs the opportunity to talk to others who have been similarly afflicted. The family requires support and strengthening so that it can optimally provide for the schizophrenic family member. Medications and specific treatments need careful monitoring and adjustment. Assessment of needs for therapy, housing, schooling, employment, socialization, and interpersonal relationships has to be an integral part of treatment. Self-esteem and motivation must be nurtured.

Schizophrenia can be a devastating disease and presents a daunting challenge, but it is one that can be dealt with successfully. When the available tools are used appropriately, and when treatment proceeds within a compassionate, hopeful, and realistic relationship, there can be important rewards for all concerned: patient, family members, and practitioner.

The helper, especially the solo helper, may well experience periods of discouragement that cannot fail to be communicated in some fashion to the patient. Our hope is that this monograph will prevent or overcome discouragement; that it may provide direction and options so that this group of deserving patients is treated sensitively, flexibly, and knowledgeably.

We thank our patients and their families for motivating us and for helping us to learn what works and what does not. Our deepest gratitude goes to Ms. Thelma Law without whom this book could not have been produced.

Mary V. Seeman
Stanley E. Greben

Chapter 1

Long-Term Nature of Treatment

STANLEY E. GREBEN, M.D., F.R.C.P.(C)

Chapter 1

Long-Term Nature of Treatment

Schizophrenia is an illness of long duration. There are those who believe that it is an illness of endless duration. In all probability, the diagnostic category includes more than one subgroup, so that with some patients who have this illness the clinician will see very little change, with others he or she will see a moderate degree of change, and with still others a great degree of change. Some patients with this diagnosis remain ill as long as they live. Others fortunately go on to lead lives that are entirely within the normal range.

There are some patients who present as schizophrenic and yet whose symptoms and signs entirely remit. These patients are in a minority, and many clinicians would, upon such a recovery, question whether or not the correct diagnosis had been made. It is not this relatively small group with which this chapter is concerned, but rather with the large majority of schizophrenic patients, with whom the duration of the difficulties presented by the illness can be measured not in months, but in years.

A practitioner who hopes to be of substantial help to such patients must have a point of view that allows him or her to persevere with treatment that is of very long duration. There is no way to avoid this, because this illness is such that it cannot be banished in a short time through focused, specific therapy. It is for this reason that many clinicians are unwilling to deal with schizophrenic patients, feeling that their treatment is wasteful and hopeless, and that as good an end result will emerge from brief, infrequent, superficial contacts with the patient. In drawing such a conclusion, the clinician loses an important opportunity to benefit not only the patient and those close to the patient, but also herself or himself. This chapter will discuss both the advantages and difficulties that can arise out of the long-term treatment of schizophrenic patients. It is the presumed difficulties that make many physicians reluctant to undertake such a therapeutic commitment.

The sources of reluctance to engage in such work lie not only in clinicians, but even more broadly in our society. Let us first examine the latter factors. Human beings during the last century have had the unique experience of rapidly finding solutions to many problems. If we need to conduct business both in North America and Europe, we can cross the Atlantic Ocean in a few hours—a far cry from the crossing of Columbus. If we contract syphilis, one injection of penicillin might very well put the infection to an end—a very different situation from that faced by people who, overwhelmed by an illness for which there was no specific therapy, ended their lives in mental hospitals, irreversibly crippled by the tertiary stage of the infection. Such successes of modern technology have induced in all of us an impatience to have problems solved rapidly and easily. Along with that attitude resides the mistaken notion that if something quick and specific cannot be done in addressing a problem, then nothing can be done. This view is shared by most groups in our society, and physicians, of course, are not free of it.

Reasons for Reluctance Toward Making Long-Term Commitments

Physicians, including psychiatrists, have various reasons for being reluctant to undertake long-term work. The first does not have to do with bad experiences with seriously ill patients, but rather with insufficient experience. Many psychiatrists have their most concentrated exposure to schizophrenic patients at the beginning of their training. Often they spend only 6

4

months or, if they are more fortunate, a year treating such patients. Contact as brief as that will usually be inadequate for the practitioner to experience the value of extended treatment of patients with a chronic illness. When a young resident sees a schizophrenic patient three or four times over a period of 6 months, prescribes medication, barely comes to know what worries the patient let alone the other host of feelings being experienced by the patient, then, not surprisingly, the resident will conclude that there is no point in seeing that patient more frequently or attempting to speak with that patient more meaningfully. When the resident becomes a psychiatrist, it is unlikely that she or he will include in her or his practice the treatment of schizophrenic patients, except when consultation or brief infrequent visits are unavoidable because of requests from colleagues or friends to whom the psychiatrist feels some sense of obligation.

The second reason that psychiatrists avoid such treatment is that they may have had some painful experience with grossly psychotic patients who, once over the more florid aspects of their illness, were all too happy to avoid further medical contacts. In these instances, the practitioner has only the opportunity to see the illness at its worst, but not the opportunity to see it at least ameliorated by ongoing contact of the patient with an informed, experienced, hopeful therapist.

The third reason for such avoidance on the part of psychiatrists is part of fashion in psychiatry. In its tendency to change with the seasons, psychiatry is no more free of fashion and favor than are most other pursuits. Psychiatry is a combination of art and science and is not so scientific as to be able to avoid swings back and forth between major attitudes. The first scientific approach to psychiatric disorders, beyond the belief in evil spirits or bad humors, was that such disorders were the result of disease of the brain. This view was superseded by the conviction that such disorders arose out of psychosocial stress, intrapsychic and intrafamilial, and that, as a result, they were best treated through specially designed social systems in hospitals and through intensive psychotherapy, including modified psychoanalysis. Then specifically effective medications became available, and something more was understood about the chemical underpinnings of such disorders, so that chemical treatment came to center stage. At about the same time, these disorders were interpreted as arising out of difficulties with social systems, so that it was expected that specifically designed community organizations could replace other more medical forms of treatment. Each of these various approaches had some validity, but none so specific as to render all other approaches unnecessary. As a consequence, despite the shifts back and forth, and the moving in and out of favor of various treatments for schizophrenia, the long-term commitment of a single clinician has remained important.

Although the medications now available (Chapters 7, 8, and 10) make extremely helpful contributions to the welfare of such patients, they do not in any way obviate the necessity of appropriate personal dealings between patient and physician. However, it is easy to understand how the swings of favor from one extreme to the other have made many practitioners feel that personal interactions with schizophrenic patients are so nonspecific as to be worth very little. Such a conclusion is far from correct. In examining the several phases through which the treatment of schizophrenia has passed, it is appropriate to mention some of those who helped establish that long-term commitment is of value.

Harry Stack Sullivan dealt with schizophrenic patients in a way that opened the door to serious personal interrelationships between therapists and their patients (Sullivan 1946). One of the most competent clinicians and writers in such matters was Frieda Fromm-Reichmann, who was able to demonstrate how some schizophrenic patients could make use of a therapist's intensive long-term commitment (Fromm-Reichmann 1954). Donald Winnicott brought the skills and attitudes of a pediatrician, modified by the insights of psychoanalysis, to similar long-term work with severely disturbed patients (Winnicott 1965). It was recognized by these and other like-minded therapists that what could be achieved of substance with those who are chronically ill can only be accomplished over an extended period of time. Younger colleagues would be well advised to read some of the writings of such pioneers; others will be referred to in Chapter 4. Whereas there can be no substitute for actual experience in doing such work, reading what has been written by those who have spent entire careers working in this field can be both enlightening and heartening to one who is contemplating engaging in similar work.

A fourth reason that long-term work with schizophrenic patients is avoided is that practitioners fear that it is not interesting or stimulating work but rather is simply a matter of making the best of a bad, even worsening situation. Such a view usually arises not out of experience but out of lack of experience. An important challenge in any psychotherapy is the patient's mistrustfulness, and hence a most significant goal that all psychotherapy must pursue is to resurrect within the patient trust in other people (Greben 1984). The same goal exists in a long-term therapeutic relationship with a schizophrenic patient, either when formal psychotherapy is engaged in or equally when the therapeutic relationship is a more medical and supportive one. In either instance the schizophrenic patient is at least as untrusting and often more so than patients who are less severely disturbed. Whatever the etiological factors of the schizophrenic illness, the patient as a person has learned to be extraordinarily cautious about relying upon other people. As a result, it takes a long time before the schizophrenic patient is willing and able to show himself or herself to the therapist. As a consequence, there may be a very long period during which the patient reveals only superficial feelings. The therapist, as a result, may need to content himself or herself with that superficiality for a long time. It is important not to be fooled by it. The clinician who believes that there is nothing more to the schizophrenic patient than the catalogue of signs and symptoms that is discernible at the outset will not be afforded the privilege of coming to know, in time, much more of that person. On the other hand, the practitioner who proceeds with caution but with steadfast persistence will probably gain the increasing confidence of the patient, and be rewarded, eventually, with the pleasure of a much fuller understanding of the patient.

It is important not to underestimate the natural timorousness of someone who is schizophrenic, for in such matters being in a hurry does not get someone to the goal more quickly. On the contrary, in such work one is more likely to get further more quickly by not hurrying at all. Niko Tinbergen, the Nobel Laureate in ethology, and his wife Elisabeth made this point in their approach to people who are autistic, and the same point can be made of working with those who are schizophrenic. The Tinbergens suggest approaching such a person the way one would approach an unfamiliar animal, let us say a dog who is a pet in a home that one is visiting. If upon seeing the dog one moves toward him in order to touch him, one may be run from by the nervous animal. If, however, the animal, when he is ready, is allowed to come and examine one, he may eventually nuzzle one's hand, at which time one may safely accept the invitation to touch, without fear of driving the animal away (Tinbergen and Tinbergen 1983). If, similarly, someone who hopes to come to know schizophrenic patients will proceed with considerable caution, and with no undue haste, then there is a good possibility that eventually the patient will develop a growing trust in the safety of dealing with the clinician. In time the patient will reveal increasingly his or her deeper thoughts and preoccupations. When this is the case, there emerge two reasons for which the therapist will find work with the schizophrenic patient more rewarding. The first is that the therapist will have gotten behind the protective screen that the patient presents to others, and have come to know aspects of an increasingly interesting person. The second is that, as a result of the physician's patience, the patient will in all likelihood begin to show some signs of clinical improvement, so that the practitioner will no longer be endlessly confronted with an unchanging clinical picture—that is, he or she will experience tangible therapeutic rewards for his or her efforts.

In short, the expectation that working over a long period

with schizophrenic patients will not be very rewarding is likely to be, for the impatient practitioner, a prophecy that fulfills itself. On the contrary, the unhurried therapist who has neither deadlines to meet nor specified goals to achieve is likely to be rewarded, in time, with work of greater interest and with therapeutic gains of a respectable magnitude.

A fifth reason for hesitation to undertake such work with schizophrenic patients is the expectation that it will be excessively demanding and will put one under severe stress all of the time. In part this opinion arises because of contacts one has had with floridly psychotic patients who have little control over their symptoms and their behavior and can be so needy and demanding. In part it arises again out of lack of experience with such patients once the more florid phase of their illness has passed.

It is true that work with schizophrenic patients is sometimes difficult, but it is not always so. In some ways working with people who are functioning at a higher social level can be more demanding. Those who are chronically ill can often be appreciative and protective of the therapist in ways that are surprising. When a fruitful working relationship of years' duration has been established, the patient, relieved that this has been possible to achieve, becomes quite protective of that which is so valued. Naturally there are times when inconvenience and overt disturbance cannot be avoided, when the usual defenses of the patient have broken down, for whatever reasons. At such times the therapist must be prepared to be available, for it is then that the patient most fears betrayal of trust and abandonment. It is unfair to expect that working with schizophrenic patients can be free of stress at all times. What I am saying, however, is that it is an unrealistic fantasy on the part of therapists that long-term work with schizophrenic patients is constantly and chronically exhausting. It is demanding work but, equally, can be most rewarding.

There is another source of concern to psychiatrists who find the prospect of such work daunting, and that is the same one that I recommended above, namely the writings of those who have made such work the principal undertaking of their long careers. Such writing is a double-edged sword: it teaches the reader a great deal because of the vast experience of the writers, but it may at the same time intimidate the reader. A good example is Harold Searles (Searles 1965). His work is characterized by the depth to which he has immersed himself in intensive, dynamically oriented psychotherapy or psychoanalysis with the most disturbed psychotic and characterologically disordered patients. The strength of his writing lies not only in the extent to which he has been willing to discuss the nature of his work, but also in the candor with which he has described his own feelings, including a host of negative ones. Searles points out how thoroughly a constant diet of such work can deplete the therapist, as he has often found himself depleted. His devotion to his patients and their welfare is admirable, as are his dedication to the truth and his frankness about those disturbing feelings that such work can stir up in a deeply involved practitioner. Unfortunately, such descriptions can serve to unduly worry less experienced therapists, making them avoid this work out of concern that their personal resources will be exhausted by it.

This brings us to the question of whether or not it is feasible to work exclusively with psychotically ill individuals. In all likelihood it is unwise to so immerse oneself in such work that one is wrung dry by it. It seems likely that practitioners should attempt to strike a balance in their work, in which they function in different ways with different types of patients who have various kinds of disorders (Greben 1989).

The concern that long-term work of this nature will be excessively demanding of the practitioner has other elements to it. One is the fear that overtly irrational patients will make unreasonable demands upon the therapist and stir up the therapist's own unconscious irrational feelings. In practice, work with schizophrenic patients is usually no more disturbed and disturbing than work with others. There will be, at times, irrational elements in the patient's productions, but not to the extent that those who are inexperienced might imagine. Much depends upon the way in which the work with the patients with schizophrenia is conducted. There have been prominent authors in the past who have recommended that the cure of psychosis is most likely to be effected by stimulating the patient to bring forward his or her deepest and most pathological feelings, in fact by provoking the patient to do so. There have also been those who, especially in the early years when phenothiazines first became available, taught that it was "papering over" the pathology to use medications and that psychopharmacologic treatment was merely "supportive" and "avoidant," as opposed to being truly therapeutic. Such a view was misguided, and practical clinical experience does not support it. There is nothing to indicate that permitting the continued existence of psychotic symptoms in order that they might be addressed or analyzed is fruitful. There is nothing to suggest that a patient benefits from being in a psychotic state or from being prodded to produce again those disturbed symptoms. On the contrary, clinical experience demonstrates the opposite. Whatever means exist to quiet the disturbed and fragmented mind should be employed. Good treatment, both short- and long-term, calms the patients, assuages their fears, and helps them to deal with their illness, their feelings, their disabilities, and the world around them. In short, working in an extended way with schizophrenic patients need not be chronically disturbing to the practitioner, since the constant thrust of the treatment should be to quiet the patient's mind as well as his or her moods and behavior.

A final source of reluctance to make such long-term commitment has to do with the long duration itself. It is intimidating to some practitioners to picture that once they have agreed to work with such a patient they will become so important, even essential to the well-being of that patient that they will have entered into an endless relationship. What is true is that the practitioner should be prepared to meet with the patient for as many years as is necessary. What is usually not correct is that throughout all those years the demands by the patient will remain the same. On the contrary, as the years pass, ordinarily

11

less and less is required of the physician. The principal reason for this is that as the patient becomes gradually convinced that he or she is in competent and caring hands, anxiety tends to diminish and what the patient needs from the clinician diminishes. As with most therapies, good enough treatment leads to a situation in which less intervention is required. On the other hand, when treatment is always insufficient or inadequate, the patient never feels fully enough responded to, and remains in great need and hence is experienced by the therapist as very demanding. If the clinician is able to give the patient a sufficient amount of what he or she needs—concern, care, attention, realistic understanding—then the patient will in all likelihood become calmer and more self-confident, and as the years pass, less will be required of the therapist by the patient. It is not only that the patient will require less emotional input on the part of the therapist. It is also that he or she will require less time. More time will ordinarily be required in the early months and years of such a working relationship in order to help the patient cope with the overwhelming feelings that assail him or her, and to get to know and be known by the physician. Often patients benefit from treatment once a week in the beginning, though of course there are many who can do with a lesser frequency. As the months and years pass it may become sufficient for the patient to be seen every 2 weeks, then once a month, and eventually only once every several months. It may seem to those who have not done such work that by the time the treatment reaches this infrequency it will be so dilute as to be serving no serious purpose. This is not the case, for once a good working partnership has been established, it benefits the patient even when patient and therapist are not together. Numerous patients have told me of an internal dialogue which they have with me between sessions. A patient whom I saw for about 4 years but have not treated for 10 years recently told me that on most days, but especially when she has difficulties, she still holds discussions with me. This patient is not now psychotic; rather these discussions are her way of carrying on the work that we began together. A rough analogy would be to compare this situation to that in which a patient exercises in order to lose weight. More calories are consumed than just in the act of exercising, for the heart rate and the metabolic rate remain elevated for some hours following the exercise. Thus the beneficial period of the treatment in both instances lasts considerably longer than the moments when the therapy is actively applied.

All patients to some measure internalize a representation of their therapists, and this applies equally to patients with schizophrenia. The effective therapist will be perceived as caring, interested, and competent, and when such an image has been internalized, it is comforting in a variety of ways. Thus long-term commitment to the care of such patients is essential and yet the continued presence of the therapist in person is not always required. The internalized representation of the therapist in the patient's mind can be a continuous source of support and help for the patient, even when the therapist is absent. However, it should be noted that such an image of a well-intentioned, helpful therapist, though it does not require the actual presence of the therapist, may very well require his or her availability, that is, potential presence. Some therapists may hesitate to make themselves too readily available, fearing that the patient will be "spoiled" into always expecting an immediate response to a call for help. This is not the case. A "spoiled" child is not the one who has had "good enough" availability of his or her mother and father. A demanding child has been insufficiently or inappropriately responded to in some ways. When a child learns that the parent is available and tends to be comforting and giving, yet at the same time knows when and how to say "no" to excessive or unnecessary demands, then in general the child requires and demands less.

In practical terms, most clinicians who treat schizophrenic patients probably make themselves available by telephone, when feasible, between office visits. As the parent must judiciously govern her or his availability, so must the therapist. Here again, there is probably undue fear that patients will abuse one's availability. When patients know that they can reach the therapist should they feel the need to do so, then most often they will not need to do so. Frequently such patients say that at a difficult time they considered calling, but knowing that the therapist could be reached was enough reassurance to get them through the difficult time. Similarly, there is a significant difference for such patients when they have a definite future appointment with the physician, even if it is not for several weeks or months, than when they do not. It is much more frightening for a patient to feel that he or she is facing the future alone than to know that at a specific time he or she will be seeing the therapist and be able to share his or her concerns.

Sources of Satisfaction for the Therapist in Making Long-Term Commitments

For the therapist who is willing to undertake the long-term treatment of patients with schizophrenia, a number of positive potential rewards exist.

The first is that these are the patients who are the most severely disordered in psychiatric terms, and whose lives, and the lives of those with whom they are closely connected, are most severely disturbed. As in all branches of medicine, one must try to help with both the minimally and the maximally ill. Society is increasingly aware of schizophrenic patients. When a clinician is able to help the most disturbed patients whom his or her specialty can address, the greatest satisfaction can be derived.

All people, including psychiatrists, carry illusions about others. Strange, other-worldly, unusual, and even bizarre people make us imagine that they are in fact different from ourselves, not only in degree, but in kind. When a clinician treats such patients he will, if he persists, eventually become increasingly aware not of their differences from himself, but of their similarities. Finding a way through to those common feelings, common attitudes, and common needs is all the more satisfying to the practitioner who has worked his or her way through a myriad of defenses. There is even more gratification for the

14

therapist in observing positive gains in a severely disturbed patient than in having that same experience with someone who was managing more adequately from the outset.

In general, the best teaching in psychiatry is done by patients. It is not their intention to teach us, but there is no source of learning available to physicians that can compare with direct experience with people who are ill. Of all our teachers, the most effective are those who are the most seriously ill. Because they have so severely and floridly come to grief, schizophrenic patients show much more of what remains hidden or obscured in all of us. Some patients of this kind illustrate psychopathology that in most other patients can only be inferred. That which is learned about these markedly impaired human beings will be of great help in our dealings with all of our patients.

The greatest satisfaction in working with patients with schizophrenia will come from the experience, over the years, of seeing someone who has been so disadvantaged become able to function more successfully in society. Surely clinicians in all branches of medicine derive the greatest rewards from helping the most severely ill patients to improve. Physicians who work in pain clinics probably derive their greatest satisfactions when they are able to help patients who are in the most pain. In the psychiatric realm, the most exquisite emotional pain is felt by our schizophrenic patients. When we are able to relieve them of some of their torment, our work has been to very good effect and will be, to ourselves, the most satisfying.

It is rewarding to understand more about the illness schizophrenia through working with such patients. Even more rewarding is to have the opportunity to know the people who are struggling with that illness. Because they feel so vulnerable, because they are so often and so easily hurt and offended, and because they have come to despair of real interest or concern on the part of others, such people are defended in awkward and complicated ways. In order to find a way through and past those defenses, the practitioner will have to be patient, persevering, and trusting. If the practitioner can be so, in time he or she is likely to be offered a fuller view of the afflicted person than most people will be permitted to have. The practitioner will get past not only the patient's mechanisms of defense, but his or her own prejudices. When it is possible to touch such an untouchable person, and to know such an unknowable person, then it is likely that the treating person will have the deepest satisfactions that his or her work is able to offer.

Quick and striking clinical achievement is not to be devalued. However, succeeding through years of careful work with a person with schizophrenia is more akin to eventually achieving the kinds of long-term personal goals that people set for themselves. Arriving at a distant destination, having managed all of the challenges en route, is rewarding in a special way—one that does not come with the arrival at nearby, more easily reached destinations.

There is one final important gratification that comes from helping patients who are schizophrenic. The illness is so debilitating that not just those who are ill are affected. When one helps the patient, therefore, one helps many people.

Thus clinicians who find their way around their fear, uncertainty, and lack of experience in order to do long-term work with patients with schizophrenia are likely to reap benefits that they will find to be among the most gratifying of their careers. These benefits will in all likelihood more than compensate for the considerable effort and creative flexibility required in the long-term treatment of schizophrenia.

References

Fromm-Reichmann F: Psychotherapy of schizophrenia. Am J Psychiatry 111:410–419, 1954

Greben SE: The re-establishment of trust through psychotherapy. Can J Psychiatry 29:350–354, 1984

Greben SE: The importance of balance in the practice of psychotherapy. Presented at the annual meeting of the Ontario Psychiatric Association, Jan 25–28, 1989

Searles HF: Collected Papers on Schizophrenia and Related

Subjects. New York, International Universities Press, 1965

Sullivan HS: Conceptions of Modern Psychiatry. Washington, DC, William Alanson White Foundation, 1946

Tinbergen N, Tinbergen EA: "Autistic" Children: New Hope for a Cure. London, George Allen & Unwin, 1983

Winnicott DW: The Maturational Process and the Facilitating Environment. New York, International Universities Press, 1965

Assessment

MARY V. SEEMAN, M.D., F.R.C.P.(C)

Chapter 2

Assessment

Accurate assessment of the patient's condition is essential in order to arrive at a working diagnosis that will lead to appropriate therapy and future planning (Hafner 1987). As the science of psychiatry advances, diagnosis will become progressively linked with etiology and pathophysiology so that therapy can become more specific and preventive measures more effective than they are at present. As the art of psychiatry advances, accurate assessment of the *person* with the diagnosis will enhance understanding and lead to more empathic interpersonal interventions.

Goals of Assessment

The initial assessment of a schizophrenic patient has as its goal the tentative answers to several questions:

- Why is this person coming today (as distinct from last month or next year)? These are the reasons for the consultation.
- What are the factors in his or her early life that have contributed to today's difficulties? (Predisposing factors)
- What are the important current factors and what are the potential consequences? (Precipitating and potentiating factors)
- What is the precise nature of the patient's difficulties, how much do they affect the person's life? (Diagnosis and severity)

- What factors influence these difficulties? (Beneficial and harmful effects)
- Who are the people in this person's life? (Social network)
- What are the important areas of this person's life: e.g., values, interests, pastimes? (Existential concerns)
- How does this person spend his or her day? (Structure of time)

The answers to these questions will not only determine the tentative diagnosis but also should provide some indications about how best to approach treatment and how to help the patient and the family to plan ahead for the future. In the course of investigating these issues, an assessment also needs to be made of the severity of the patient's illness, the need for hospitalization, the potential for aggressive behavior or suicidal behavior, and the patient's mental competency with respect to both treatment decisions and the management of personal affairs.

Why Is This Person Here Today?

Most frequently, the individual with schizophrenia does not come alone but is accompanied by a concerned or frustrated parent who arranged for the psychiatric assessment. Contrary to other conditions where the individual recognizes that he or she is ill and needs help, the person with schizophrenic symptoms characteristically does not recognize this. He or she may be aware that something is wrong but does not view the ailment as a medical disease. The patient's relationship with the family often determines the timing of the assessment.

Example
The patient was Jim—a well-groomed young man who, however, was dressed in shorts in the middle of a Canadian winter. He was angry and sarcastic, especially toward his aunt, who had accompanied him. He spoke of numerous injustices that had been done to him but it was not possible to piece together the story of his life. He spoke of numerous hospital admissions in

the past. When his aunt was asked to join us, she told me that Jim's behavior was essentially unchanged over the last year, that he had always been difficult to live with but that the reason she was coming now was because Jim's mother, her sister, had had a heart attack. The mother was recovering in the hospital and the aunt was now alone with Jim. She was unable to visit her sister in the hospital and care for Jim at the same time. She was hoping that I might be able to hospitalize him.

Understanding the many interlocking reasons why a long-standing problem has come to a head is a crucial aspect of the assessment. It is often the main reason why the psychiatrist is being consulted.

What Are Early Life Factors?

Example

Sylvia was diagnosed as suffering from schizophrenia after a suicide attempt in which she stepped into traffic deliberately because her voices told her that the Mafia was looking for her and would torture her and eventually kill her. Her early life was significant to her story. She was born the illegitimate daughter of a nightclub dancer. She never knew her father but gathered that he was from a background very different from her mother's. She was brought up by her grandparents because her mother was unstable and not consistently there. Mother, maternal grandmother, and maternal uncle were all hospitalized with psychiatric illness, probably schizophrenia. The factors that marked Sylvia's early life were her genetic heritage, her illegitimacy, and the feeling that half of her had a completely different heritage. Also significant was the absence of consistent caretakers other than her grandfather. What saved her in childhood from early psychiatric disease were her cleverness, her extreme good looks, and her ease of learning, which made her popular at school with friends and teachers.

Factors that are known to predispose to schizophrenia are genetics, low birth weight, birth complications, winter birth, neurologic difficulties, shyness in girls, and school problems in boys (Hare 1975; Kendler and Hays 1982; Lewis and Murray 1987; Parnas 1986; Watt 1974).

What Are Later Life Factors?

Example
Sylvia's story was that her grandfather attempted to have intercourse with her when she was in her early teens and then hung himself in the basement of the home they shared when she was 15. Sylvia was the person who found him and who was charged with the funeral arrangements. The person who helped her was an older Italian man, who was divorced and who took an interest in her and made sure that she finished school. He was the first person with whom Sylvia had sexual relations; she married him when she was 19 and began to look after him and his young son. She suspected that he had dealings with the Mafia but ignored this at first because she was able to live in style and felt pampered. As the years went by, she realized that her husband was secretive and very jealous, and she began to feel more and more imprisoned in the house. He did not let her go anywhere alone. The only man she could see privately was her doctor, and she developed a fantasy that she was in love with the doctor and he with her. The precipitant to her hearing the voices that led to the suicide attempt was the doctor's denial that he felt anything for her other than professional caring.

Life difficulties that may precipitate schizophrenia are many, among which are drug abuse, poverty, physical trauma, prolonged illness, and a hostile and intrusive family life (Schulsinger et al. 1987; Vaughn et al. 1985).

What Is the Precise Nature of These Difficulties?

Characteristic difficulties in schizophrenia are bizarre delusions with no basis in reality whatsoever. In Sylvia's case, the delusion of being poisoned and tortured by the Mafia appeared at first bizarre but, in fact, had a basis in reality because her husband was a jealous man and *was* connected with the Mafia.

Many years later, Sylvia's husband, whom she had long since divorced, in fact killed his third wife, Sylvia's successor, in a fit of jealousy.

Delusions that are characteristic of schizophrenia are those involving somatic sensations and convictions of body change, grandiose delusions of being famous or assuming the identity of a historical figure, excessive religious preoccupations, false convictions, ideas of annihilation, and belief in the world's coming to an imminent end. Phenomena considered implausible within the person's culture take on this quality of bizarreness. Persecutory delusions or false convictions that spouse or partner is unfaithful are so common that, in themselves, they do not qualify as symptoms of schizophrenia unless they are accompanied, as in the case of Sylvia, by hallucinations, incoherence, catatonic behavior, or flat/inappropriate affect.

Hallucinations are usually auditory in schizophrenia. They may take the form of a voice commenting on the behavior or the thinking of the patient. In order to qualify as schizophrenic hallucinations, the voices must be frequent and repetitive and must contain more than one or two words. Mood-incongruent voices, two or more voices talking with each other, or voices keeping up a constant commentary, even when unaccompanied by other symptoms, point to schizophrenia. Incoherence of speech is also characteristic of schizophrenia; thoughts appear illogical or there is a scarcity of thought. When this is accompanied either by flat or inappropriate affect, delusions or hallucinations, or catatonic behavior, it qualifies for a diagnosis of schizophrenia. Jim, of the first example, qualifies on the basis of a string of illogical thought associations accompanied by disorganized behavior. He probably also held a variety of delusions but it was impossible to substantiate these on the first interview, and he denied hearing voices or having visual, somatic, or tactile hallucinations.

To summarize, DSM-III-R requires the presence of 1), 2), or 3):

1. Two of the following:
   Delusions
   Prominent hallucinations
   Incoherence of thought
   Catatonic behavior
   Flat or inappropriate affect
2. Bizarre delusions alone
3. Prominent hallucinations that are incongruent with mood, a voice that keeps up a running commentary on the person, or two or more voices conversing.

These symptoms must be present for at least a week (unless vigorous treatment stops them earlier).

The diagnosis of schizophrenia also requires the demonstration of a deterioration of functioning in relation to work, social relations, and/or self-care. The duration of illness must be at least 6 months before a diagnosis of schizophrenia can be made. A similar syndrome lasting less than 6 months would be called schizophreniform, and judgment as to eventual outcome would be reserved.

During the 6 months in which the illness is present, the active symptoms may disappear but they must be there for at least a week and the person must experience prodromal or residual symptoms for the remainder of the 6 months in order for the diagnosis to be firm. Exclusion criteria include the presence of an organic mental state (Hayes 1985). This may need to be ruled out by neurological examination, neurocognitive tests, EEG, MRI, or CT scan. Lack of response to standard neuroleptic treatment is an indication for thorough biochemical and neurological screening, if this has not been done initially. Residual symptoms (which may also be prodromal) are social isolation; difficulties in maintenance of social role (student, housewife, worker); eccentric behavior; inattention to personal hygiene or appearance; flat or inappropriate affect; vague, tangential, circumstantial, or metaphoric speech; magical thinking; strange ideas; ideas of reference; overvalued ideas;

illusions; and depersonalization phenomena. The presence of two of these symptoms is necessary to qualify as prodromal or residual. If these symptoms exist alone without a week-long period of active symptoms, the diagnosis is schizotypal personality (Goldstein 1983).

Other than organic states, one must eliminate from consideration a factitious psychosis and a brief reactive psychosis (brought on by an extremely stressful event). Schizoaffective psychosis and mood disorder with psychotic features need to be ruled out before a diagnosis of schizophrenia is made (Kendell and Brockington 1980). Affective syndromes, brief reactive psychoses, schizophreniform illness, and schizotypal personality have a better prognosis than schizophrenia and need to be considered first (Cloninger et al. 1985). Characteristically, schizophrenia has a profound effect on the whole of the person's life (school, work, interpersonal relations, leisure, self-esteem). Where symptoms occupy only a corner of the person's life, delusional disorders should be considered. The working diagnosis cannot help but influence the therapist's prognosis. It therefore requires deliberation and should be offered sensitively to both patient and family. The maintenance of hope for a successful outcome is always important but, at the same time, unrealistic expectation must be avoided. If diagnosis is uncertain, as it frequently is, judgment is reserved and patients and families are given the range of diagnostic possibilities. Specific diagnosis may not be realistic until a year or more has elapsed.

What Makes Schizophrenic Symptoms Better and Worse?

Schizophrenia runs a fluctuating course, and the reasons for remissions and relapses are often unclear. Also unclear is why the illness is so much more serious in some individuals than in others. Poverty, lack of social supports, low intelligence, birth difficulties, early onset, neurological problems, a nonparanoid form of the illness, drug and alcohol abuse, being male, evidence of brain atrophy on CT scan, hostility and criticism at home, difficulties in controlling aggressive urges, poor premorbid skills and adjustment, failure to adhere to a treatment program, and lack of response to antipsychotic medication are all associated with deterioration. Deterioration is characterized by more and longer hospitalizations, more self-harm, more unemployment, and social isolation. Being female, left-handedness, affective coloring to the illness, good object relations, good cognitive skills, older age of onset, marriage, and the paranoid form of the illness are associated with a better prognosis, characterized by fewer hospitalizations, lower dosage of antipsychotic drugs, and a better quality of life (Cloninger et al. 1985; Seeman 1986; Strauss and Carpenter 1974).

Who Are the Significant People in This Person's Life?

The person's social network and its extent, closeness, and ability to support the patient both instrumentally and emotionally in times of stress are crucial to the course the illness will take. The patient's ability to maintain relations with family and friends and the quality of those relations will determine, to some extent, the quality of the bond that is possible between therapist and patient and will prove to be the key to the patient's treatability.

What Are the Important Areas of the Patient's Life?

The ability to work, to be creative, or to maintain active interest in sports, literature, films, or friendships is another key to treatment. Political commitment or spiritual faith may be the determining factor. Although apathy and lack of motivation accompany many schizophrenias, an active, interested premorbid life is a good indication that interest in living can be revived.

How Does the Person Spend His or Her Day?

Because many schizophrenic patients are reluctant to speak at all and are especially reluctant to talk about symptoms, one of the better ways of engaging them in conversation and also of discovering what motivates them and what frightens them is to ask how they spend a typical day. More often than not the interviewer will learn that the patient sleeps late, rarely showers or brushes his or her teeth, rarely cleans his or her room or makes the bed, usually does not take part in meal preparation or washing up, spends the day watching TV or simply "doing nothing," avoids the rest of the family, sees few friends, and does not go out of the house except at night. There are variations on this pattern, but a description of the structure of the day will illuminate fears that suggest delusional thinking. ("I don't go out because I don't want the neighbors to see me." "I don't answer the phone because it is tapped." "I don't watch TV because they try to involve me in the program.") The pattern of the day will also point to areas of probable friction with parents or siblings. ("I don't do the dishes; I leave that to my sister." "I don't eat until my mother comes home from work and prepares supper." "I don't wash my clothes; my mother does it eventually." "I stay up all night playing the radio.")

Need for Collateral History

Very often, the same question, "How do you spend your day?", will elicit different answers from the patient and from the parent. Again, the discrepancy is important to note since the patient may have a very different idea of himself or herself than that held by the family. A patient may say "I have very many good friends and we talk on the phone all the time." The mother or father of this person could very well say that the patient used to have very many good friends in high school but that for many years has refused to see anyone and that, these days, the friends only call at Christmas or on the patient's birthday. The patient's perception of himself or herself frequently antedates the illness. A patient may still think of himself as he was then and may seem to be marking time until the old times return.

The parent's or significant other's description of changes in the patient and of his or her present-day behavior is an important part of the assessment. When the interviewer has access only to the patient's subjective report, it is extremely difficult to distinguish between reality and wishful thinking on the part of the patient. Much is denied or forgotten, and there is too little evidence upon which to form a sound diagnostic opinion. One often guesses that there are areas about which the patient does not talk—often this is made clear by, for example, the expression of the patient's eyes. Although educated guesses on the part of the examiner are frequently valid, they may not be, so that diagnostic impressions cannot be based on them (Schwartz and Wiggins 1987). Patients from other cultures or from social classes removed from the examiner's own may convey undecodable nonverbal messages and often such individuals are mistakenly given a diagnosis of schizophrenia. The original mistaken diagnosis may stay with them for many years and be reconfirmed without thorough reassessment over time. It is important, therefore, to diagnose officially only on the basis of information that is substantiated and to relegate hunches and guesses to the back of one's mind until after investigations are complete or after the patient trusts the doctor enough to recount the full story.

Example

I was asked to assess a young man who had come to the emergency department a few days earlier in a panic, claiming that he was being followed and would be killed. On careful questioning, the young man said nothing that could be construed as psychotic. He had various somatic symptoms about which he spoke. He had trouble sleeping, and he felt stressed by the demands of schoolwork. He agreed to come for regular visits because he felt isolated, had few friends, and was inept with girls. His mother and brother were also interviewed, and they mentioned instances of erratic behavior that sounded serious but that the patient said he did not remember. The diagnosis was left open, and the patient was treated with a low dose of antipsychotic medication and with supportive therapy. Six months later, he told me this complex story: at the time I started to see him, he was being followed by government agents, Russians or CIA. They were following him not from behind but in front so that he would see them and know what they were doing and get frightened. Their motive was to frighten him and then to observe how a frightened human being responds. They knew how he responded because they could read minds. They had selected him because he frightened easily and because he was smart so that he, predictably, put into effect a "spy operation" to find out who these people were and to fend them off. They knew he was doing this, and it was his response that they were interested in because it would be good training for their agents. In other words, they made him "paranoid" so that they could learn from his paranoia how to be good spies. He knew this to be true because he heard people on the subway talking of "the secret police." He heard these words in his own head but they were not his thoughts because they were said in a foreign voice. So the voices must have been implanted thoughts from the people sitting next to him. He saw men, dressed in T-shirts with foreign writing on them that must have been Russian, lounging around his doorway. The phone rang and when he picked it up he heard gibberish that must have been Russian and then whoever it was hung up. He always had to be a step ahead of these people. They also told him he would be in trouble if he told anyone so he never did until now. He was a little afraid in telling me for fear of what might happen but he believed that for some time they must have found another target because they were leaving him alone. He felt they left him alone because he had learned to "blank his mind," which meant that they could no longer read any thoughts he had and he was no longer useful to them.

This is a good illustration of an elaborate delusional system that the patient continued to believe in after obvious symptoms had waned and that he could not discuss when his illness was acute.

The Need for Regular Reassessment

In the course of time, patients' pathology may change (Caine and Shoulson 1983). They may reveal more so that it is easier to make a more valid diagnosis or they may develop new symptoms or, by the same token, lose some prominent symptoms altogether. Very frequently what seems at first to be a schizophrenic illness develops into an affective one, and this happens in the other direction as well. The degree of symptom discomfort needs reassessment as do the patient's relationships, capacity for work or retraining, and plans for the future. None of these are static. The danger is to treat a chronic illness as if it were always the same and not to pay attention to changing symptoms, changing capabilities, changing needs. When conducting consultations for family physicians who are treating individuals with schizophrenia, it is wise to suggest an annual or biannual reassessment. Even during a plateau period of illness, antipsychotic dosages need to be reevaluated regularly. Failure to respond to treatment may require the determination of neuroleptic blood levels or the search for missed primary or secondary diagnoses.

Assessing the Family

An extensive inquiry into the family's history of psychiatric disease will help to establish the patient's genetic liability to schizophrenic illness (Schulsinger et al. 1987). In addition, since it is the family who provides primary care, it is important to assess their strengths and weaknesses and to offer individual help or family help as required. Family members may need assistance with individual problems or they may need support and education around the needs of the schizophrenic relative. Again, these needs are not static and should be reevaluated over time (see Chapter 5 on family treatment).

Classification of Illness

Diagnosis has been a controversial area in psychiatry (Schwartz and Wiggins 1987). There continue to exist a number of different systems of classification although the official system of the American Psychiatric Association, DSM-III-R, is the one in current use in North America (Goldstein 1983). This system, evolving from DSM-III and Feighner's research criteria, owes its concept of schizophrenia mainly to Kraepelin, who differentiated dementia praecox from other psychoses on the basis of early onset, downhill course, and poor prognosis. The concept of poor prognosis has not always applied to schizophrenia and continues to be a subject of controversy. Long-term follow-up studies suggest that, even using the DSM-III classification scheme, many schizophrenic patients recover as they age. Bleuler's system, characterized by difficulties in association of thought and of affect with characteristic autistic tendencies and ambivalence, did not necessarily carry a poor prognosis. It offered more hope for therapeutic interventions and placed emphasis on thought disorder above other symptoms. DSM-III-R includes thought disorder as an important symptom but does not attribute to it prime diagnostic significance.

Ego psychology is based on the assessment of ego functions, and schizophrenia is defined as a defect in reality testing, sense of reality, and adaptation to reality. It is further characterized as a defect in the regulation and control of sexual and aggressive drives and as a defect in the processing of thought. There are concomitant disturbances in object relations—the tendencies to use others in order to meet one's own needs and to distort the other in accordance to one's own needs. Defensive functions in schizophrenia are said to be primitive: projection, introjection and denial, fragmentation, disintegration, splitting, fusion, and a defect in repression so that patients often speak of topics normally censored. They are therefore perceived as regressed. Orientation, memory, and intellectual processes are frequently left intact. This is important to note when making a differential diagnosis. The synthetic function of the ego is defective, producing the perplexity and confusion that are the hallmark of many individuals with schizophrenia. The ego psychology system is helpful for therapeutic interventions but has not been integrated into DSM-III-R.

Schneider's first rank symptoms (hearing own thoughts, auditory hallucinations in the form of a running commentary or two voices conversing, thought withdrawal, thought insertion, thought broadcasting, somatic hallucinations, delusional perception, delusion of influence) have been incorporated into DSM-III-R, and schizophrenia is now commonly understood as a disease of ego boundaries. Other systems in use are the New Haven Schizophrenic Index, Carpenter and Strauss's Flexible Criteria, the Feighner criteria, and the Research Diagnostic Criteria (RDC). As mentioned, the latter two were the precursors of DSM-III.

Previous American systems (DSM-I and DSM-II) were based more on ego psychology and Bleuler. They allowed a broad definition of schizophrenia that included both good and bad prognosis. DSM-III is a departure, in line with Feighner and RDC, a return to the relatively narrow definition of Kraepelin that assumes a bleak outlook for schizophrenia (Goldstein 1983).

Classifications are efforts to provide a common language for practitioners talking about patients in groups. They are useful in that roughly the same types of patients are placed in specific categories and any two physicians are now more likely to give the same individual similar diagnoses. These diagnostic groupings facilitate trials of therapy that can be varied in order to produce maximum improvement in homogeneous samples of patients (Schwartz and Wiggins 1987). In this respect they are helpful. It is tempting, however, to consider diagnostic systems as defining a specific illness with a specific etiology and treatment response and outcome. This is not so, and individual differences continue to exist within large groupings. Treatment interventions are most successful when they are geared to the individual rather than to the diagnostic group to which the individual belongs.

Standardized Interviews

Although clinicians usually develop their own style of interviewing which varies from patient to patient, structured interviews are becoming more popular. They aid reliability and can be computerized to yield diagnostic impressions "objectively" (Helzer 1983). Structured interviews ask the same questions to each patient in the same order. The wording of each question is predetermined, the same probe is used for individual symptoms, and the information is recorded in a uniform manner. Structured interviews are now used ubiquitously for research purposes where their value is acknowledged, although it is recognized that the patient may either deny or forget events to the extent that his or her answers do not approximate the objective facts. In clinical work, structured interviews are cumbersome because much time may be used in pursuing avenues that do not apply to that particular patient. Spontaneous reporting of a symptom gives it more clinical meaning than a simple endorsement of a symptom suggested by the examiner. On the other hand, there is no question that clinical information thus obtained is usually more complete and more consistent than that gleaned from an unstructured, free-floating interview. In an unstructured situation, the clinician may be overinfluenced by presenting symptoms and neglect to probe other important areas. The use of structured questions does not need to be wooden and should elicit the same rapport with the patient as the more unstructured clinical interview. Either one, to be effective, needs to be practiced and to become spontaneous. For some disorganized schizophrenic patients there is comfort in a very orderly interview that proceeds from one area to the next in a way that structures the patient's time frame and makes it evident that the symptoms asked about are commonplace and frequently occurring. This may be very comforting to the patient who is afraid that his or her psychotic "vibes" are being picked up by the examiner and that questions are selected that are specific to him or her.

As time goes on, structured interviewing, made flexible by the experience and personal style of the interviewer, will probably become more common in office practice. Although there exist standardized interviews that do not need to be administered by a skilled clinician, these will probably not invade clinical practice but will remain an epidemiologic tool for the screening of large populations (Helzer 1983).

Clinicians must remember that there is no magic in computer-generated diagnoses derived from structured interviews. The diagnostic impression that results from these is as fallible as a clinical one, in some ways more so and in other ways less so. Whatever the method of producing a diagnosis, it is always tentative and approximate and requires periodic reassessment in order to ensure optimal therapeutic interventions.

References

Caine ED, Shoulson I: Psychiatric syndromes in Huntington's disease. Am J Psychiatry 140:728–733, 1983

Cloninger CR, Martin RL, Guze SB, et al: Diagnosis and prognosis in schizophrenia. Arch Gen Psychiatry 42:15–25, 1985

Goldstein WN: DSM-III and the diagnosis of schizophrenia. Am J Psychother 37:168–181, 1983

Hafner H: The concept of disease in psychiatry (editorial). Psychol Med 17:11–14, 1987

Hare HE: Season of birth in schizophrenia and neurosis. Am J Psychiatry 132:1168–1171, 1975

Hayes P: Implications of the distinction between organic and functional psychoses. Acta Psychiatr Scand 71:620–625, 1985

Helzer JE: Standardized interviews in psychiatry. Psychiatr

Dev 2:161–178, 1983

Kendell RE, Brockington IF: The identification of disease entities and the relationship between schizophrenic and affective psychosis. Br J Psychiatry 137:324–331, 1980

Kendler K, Hays P: Familial and sporadic schizophrenia: a symptomatic, prognostic and EEG comparison. Am J Psychiatry 139:1557–1562, 1982

Lewis SW, Murray RM: Obstetric complications, neurodevelopmental deviance, and risk of schizophrenia. J Psychiatr Res 21:413–421, 1987

Parnas J: Risk factors in the development of schizophrenia: contributions from a study of children of schizophrenic mothers. Danish Med Bull 33:127–133, 1986

Schulsinger F, Parnas J, Mednick S, et al: Heredity environment interaction and schizophrenia. J Psychiatr Res 21:431–436, 1987

Schwartz MA, Wiggins OP: Typifications: the first step for clinical diagnosis in psychiatry. J Nerv Ment Dis 175:65–77, 1987

Seeman MV: Current outcome in schizophrenia: women vs men. Acta Psychiatr Scand 73:609–617, 1986

Strauss J, Carpenter W: The prediction of outcome in schizophrenia. Arch Gen Psychiatry 31:37–42, 1974

Vaughn CE, Snyder KS, Jones S, et al: Family factors in schizophrenic relapse. Arch Gen Psychiatry 41:1169–1177, 1985

Watt NF: Patterns of social development in adult schizophrenia. Arch Gen Psychiatry 35:160–165, 1974

Chapter 3

Engaging Patient and Family in Treatment

MARY V. SEEMAN, M.D., F.R.C.P.(C)

Chapter 3

Engaging Patient and Family in Treatment

Because it can be achieved only with time and in the context of a consistent, trustworthy relationship, treating the schizophrenic patient requires a long-term commitment from the patient and from the therapist.

Engaging the patient in such a commitment is a complex task (Greben 1981, 1987). Typically, the patient wants little to do with psychiatry and prefers to view the illness from a short-term perspective. The longitudinal view of life, of illness, or of treatment is frightening (Anonymous 1986). The successful engagement of the schizophrenic patient in long-term therapy can be divided into relational, expectational, communicational, affective, and technical components (Docherty and Fiester 1985).

Patient-Doctor Relationship

An alliance must be forged with a relatively unwilling patient and must be built on a foundation that will survive repeated crises over long periods of time (Werman 1981). Agreement needs to be reached in the initial period about the rules that will govern therapy, that is, the frequency of sessions, attendance and fees for missed appointments, telephone contact between therapy hours, family involvement, the use of drugs, the use of cotherapists, the availability of emergency rooms for crises, and the possibility of hospitalization. As these issues are negotiated at the beginning of therapy, conflicts of authority

41

among the three usual protagonists—the patient, the therapist, and the family—quickly emerge. The therapist's task is to promote active participation and collaboration (Adler 1985). In other words, the therapist must be prepared to surrender the role of sole expert and to acknowledge that the patient from his or her perspective, and the family from theirs, are also experts in the condition that is being treated.

The psychiatrist needs to be flexible enough initially to allow the patient and family to set the frequency of meetings (Camenietzki and Albott 1976). The patient usually wants to meet infrequently at first. He or she relishes the freedom of being able to set the date of the next appointment and takes pleasure in keeping the doctor waiting and in terminating the interview on impulse. In a crisis, on the other hand, the patient insists on being seen immediately and resents being kept waiting. In other words, schizophrenic patients, characteristically, feel the need to overcome their sense of extreme powerlessness by being able to exert illusory power over the relationship with their doctor (Searles 1967). In the initial alliance stage, utmost flexibility on the part of the doctor cements the relationship and allows this balance-of-power behavior to be explored together and to be understood. The doctor is limited in his or her flexibility and the patient knows that. The patient needs some confirmation, however, that the doctor is willing to negotiate and that small sacrifices will be made in order to accommodate particular needs (Tuma et al. 1978). The demands of the family are often more difficult to accommodate and may be experienced by the therapist as more importunate in that the family is not seen as powerless. There are many difficulties in negotiating dominance-subordination around the various therapy issues among three parties whose views are different and strongly held (Munich 1987; Werman 1981). One way is to allow each party to have the "say" for a period of time, specified in advance, and then to transfer that authority to the next party. In this sense, allowing the patient to take authority initially is recommended, titrating this as needed.

Missed appointments are commonplace. My own routine

is to always have other work available so that I do not feel rejected by and resentful of the patient. If the patient comes late, I see him or her briefly and make another appointment to fully discuss his or her issues. If the patient does not come, I telephone and offer a new appointment time. If I think it will help, I invite the patient to come with a relative or a friend. Sometimes it turns out that it is the hour of the appointment that is the main deterrent—too early, or during rush hour, or at a time when the patient might meet someone in the hall whom he or she is trying to avoid. Many times I allow patients to skip visits and maintain our relationship by telephone. Sometimes this leads nowhere but at times, after a few telephone sessions, patients have appeared for the next and subsequent appointments.

Example
Wilma was not a new patient but as her illness fluctuated and as circumstances changed, our relationship experienced many new beginnings. These were always tumultuous and marked by many missed appointments. We devised a scheme whereby I kept a set time for her every week, whether or not she came. When she did not come, I left her a note pinned to my door. The note contained her week's prescription and the date of her next appointment. Invariably, after a day or two, the note disappeared. She would come when she knew I was not there, take the note, and leave. At other times, she came for the note and sat and waited for me, even when it was not her "time." She knew then that we would barely manage to have time to exchange greetings. I realized that she actually preferred these brief exchanges to the longer times that were reserved for her. The relative impersonality of the notes and the brief "hellos" in the waiting room may have been easier to tolerate than the regular appointments, face-to-face in my office.

Expectations

It is important that there be congruence between the goals of patient, family, and therapist (Adler 1985). This is not easy to achieve but is easier if long-term goals are scaled. The achievement of each new level, in itself unnoteworthy, solidifies the

43

relationship and allows progression toward the end points that all three parties hope to achieve. Strupp (1969) describes the "lessons" that psychotherapy ultimately teaches. These lessons are as valid for the schizophrenic patient as for any other even though the patient or the family may initially view them skeptically. These lessons are:

1. The world is not such a bad place after all, and people are in general trustworthy and reliable. For the schizophrenic person, this is a lesson that will take much time to learn and that will be repeatedly forgotten. A first-level shared goal might be to experience the "world" of the therapist's office as safe and reliable.
2. One has to be less demanding of people. The family will see this as a worthwhile goal since the schizophrenic family member is frequently excessively demanding of them and they may be feeling exploited and resentful. The patient views this from a different perspective but may agree to the first-level goal of transferring the demands and unmet needs from family to psychiatrist. In time, he or she will learn to temper the demands and eventually to meet some of the needs autonomously.
3. One cannot expect others to praise one's successes. This is a difficult lesson in general and perhaps an impossible one for the schizophrenic patient who requires consistent praise in order to continue with activities that are difficult for him or her to initiate. For most individuals, the inherent pleasure of accomplishment permits the praise of others to matter less. For the patient with schizophrenia, pleasure is a fleeting experience so that the appreciation of others takes on proportionately greater importance. The therapist teaches the family, by deed as well as by discussion, the importance of consistently praising and applauding tasks successfully accomplished by the patient.
4. One must learn to delay gratification. This is a lesson that in some ways the schizophrenic patient has already

learned. His or her imaginations and delusions can be conceptualized as substitute gratifications. These particular techniques have to be unlearned and other, more functional substitutes found. In essence, therapy in its minute-to-minute conduct teaches delays and postponements and substitutions in the sense that wishes are not immediately understood and positive reinforcement not immediately forthcoming. The lesson of the therapist to the schizophrenic patient is that when frustrations arise, there are options to pursue that ultimately serve better than a flight into psychotic thinking.

5. Separation is painful but it is still worthwhile to embark on relationships. This is a particularly difficult lesson for the schizophrenic patient who has learned to avoid people because of the pain of termination. It is for this reason that long-term commitment is necessary in the treatment of the schizophrenic patient and many gains can be made in the successful resolution of reactions to therapist vacations.

6. Sitting back and wishing is not likely to produce results. This is another particularly difficult lesson for the schizophrenic patient who finds realistic effort toward a specific goal very difficult to undertake. This is a long-term goal probably best avoided initially.

7. Avoidance of suffering is ultimately self-defeating. The pain of suffering in schizophrenia is sometimes overwhelming and at times may need to be avoided at all costs. How much pain can be tolerated is a matter of trial and error that the collaborative work between patient and therapist eventually clarifies.

8. Certain interpersonal maneuvers are self-defeating. The person with schizophrenia, like everyone else, displays habitual patterns of behavior with others, some of which result in extra difficulties. When the patient is in remission, therapeutic work can illuminate behavior patterns and help change those that need changing. These are long-term goals, which the patient will get to later in treatment.

9. Cooperation pays off. The therapist assists the learning of this important lesson by treating the patient and the family as equals, which fosters cooperation.

10. There is a distinction between feelings and actions. Feelings need to be acknowledged and explored but one is responsible for one's actions and these cannot be excused by illness. This is a critical lesson, especially in schizophrenia where feelings are sometimes murderous. The patient may want "to be rid of" these feelings. The lesson is to tolerate the feelings without yielding to the impulse to discharge them inappropriately. This is a goal that in various forms can be shared and agreed upon by patient, therapist, and family.

11. One must stand up for one's legitimate rights. This lesson is particularly important for those patients who are fearful and passive. Legitimate rights within the treatment situation need to be recognized by both patient and therapist.

12. One needs to accept certain kinds of authority. This is inevitable in a family, at school, or at work, and this lesson also can be learned within the treatment situation itself.

13. Despite the above, the existence of freedoms needs to be acknowledged. The schizophrenic patient may form a symbiosis with the therapist or with a family member and needs to experience the freedom of loosening that bond. If the bond is with a family member, both partners of the bondage may resist freeing it. This, then, becomes a difficult lesson to impart.

14. One needs to accept that the future is in one's hands. Within limits, this is true for the schizophrenic patient although, frequently, his or her future is severely limited by the illness. One major therapeutic task is the instilling of hope.

15. One needs to establish a flexible but recognizable identity. Too often, the identity achieved for the schizophrenic patient is the sick role. The family may or may not encourage this but the therapist needs constantly to point out aspects of the person's identity that are not affected by his illness.

Communication

Comprehensibility is an important issue. The patient is frequently difficult to understand and, unconsciously, the lack of clarity impinges on the doctor and may render him or her equally vague and unclear. In the course of therapy with schizophrenic patients, I have from time to time pulled back from our conversation and wondered what the effect of what we were saying to each other would have on a neutral observer. McGlashan (1982, 1983; Keats and McGlashan 1985) makes the point that therapists of schizophrenic individuals need to be "a little crazy." He means, I think, "interested in craziness" or empathic to it. It is not, however, helpful to the patient for the therapist to glide into the same vagueness and incoherence that sometimes characterize the patient's speech. It is important that whatever the therapist says be brief, explicit, jargon free, and easily understandable. Instructions as to future appointments or goals between appointments or prescriptions for medications and how to take them all need to be repeated many times and, preferably, written. Instructions need to be given one at a time, not en masse.

Much time should be spent acknowledging the communication of the patient. That is difficult when the patient is being unclear. Initially, it is perhaps not wise to continually ask what he means or ask him to say it in another way or rephrase what he has said. At the beginning, quiet listening, acknowledgment of the importance of what is being said, and attempts to answer queries clearly is all that is required. Although much has been written about the benefits and possible risks of silence (McGlashan 1983), a comfortable silence on the part of the therapist is often very well tolerated. Ideally it should communicate comfort with the patient and with the patient's words or lack of them. Since it may, however, be perceived as helplessness or hostility, signs of interest and enjoyment of the patient's company need to be transmitted somehow, verbally or nonverbally. This may be in the form of leaning forward or nodding or simply stating, "Please tell me more, I don't know you well enough yet to ask the right questions. As I get to know you better, this will change." If the patient is silent, one can say, "I don't mind you being quiet, as long as it's restful for you." Or, if the patient is communicating nonverbal signs of distress, "It is probably difficult to talk to a relative stranger. We can make this a short meeting and as we get to know each other better, it will be easier to talk."

Families, in particular, have many questions for the doctor and sometimes these need to be answered several times. The phenomenon of asking the same question repeatedly, as if it had not already been asked and answered, can be irritating to the doctor and can inhibit effective communication. This phenomenon needs to be understood. It is not that the family (or patient) has not heard or has not remembered. It is either that more reassurance is needed or, on the other hand, if the answer has been disturbing (to do with diagnosis or prognosis or need for medication, for instance), that more time is needed to absorb it and to adapt to it (Anonymous 1986).

Example
The Gurneys asked for a second opinion about their son, Barney. He was being seen by another psychiatrist but they felt the diagnosis was unconfirmed and wanted some directions about medication. The treating psychiatrist told me that he saw son and family very frequently and that they asked essentially the same questions many times. He felt that having someone else answer their questions would help. I spent several hours with Barney and his parents. They had many questions, individually and collectively. These had to do with the nature of the treatment Barney had received, the possibility of a hereditary component to the illness, and, most important, they were looking for suggestions on how to manage Barney's symptoms at home.

These were all valid questions that they claimed had not been addressed by the treating psychiatrist. Since the psychiatrist was on holiday, I agreed to see them during his time away because they were undergoing a period of great distress. During this time, they called me repeatedly at work and at home, trying to specify what exactly I had said. They continued to do this after their psychiatrist had returned, so after consulting with him, I told them that he would answer their questions and that it would be less confusing if the answers came from one source only. Several months went by and I heard from the Gurneys again. Their psychiatrist was again on vacation and—according to them—had not left anyone to take his calls. Again they asked essentially the same questions. I found out subsequently that not only had the psychiatrist left someone to replace him, but that the Gurneys had also made appointments with two other psychiatrists, again asking the same questions.

This is a good example of how tortured and torturing a family can be when the diagnosis of schizophrenia is first made and when treatment does not progress as well as they had hoped. They find it very hard to adapt to a new reality and need constant reassurance that all that is possible is being done, that there is nothing they can do that they are not already doing, and that no one has made an error of diagnosis. Behind that is a magical fantasy that everyone is wrong and that their son will be well after all, without medicines and without the prolonged treatment that the experts are recommending. Because these kinds of family reactions may be perceived by the therapist as undermining or devaluating, it is often difficult to sustain the therapeutic relationship through this initial period of questioning. It is, however, only a stage that the threesome (patient, family, and therapist) can successfully navigate by solidifying their relationship and anchoring the alliance through the development of mutual trust.

Affective Tone

Nonverbal communication is especially important in schizophrenia because the patient is quick to interpret every smile, every stifled yawn, every movement, and every change in tone. This is especially so at the beginning when the therapist's tics and habitual gestures are not yet familiar. It is crucial to realize that when a new patient stops talking or appears distressed or frightened or laughs inappropriately, it is frequently a reaction to his interpretation of what the therapist has communicated nonverbally. For instance, a smile may signify ridicule, blowing one's nose may mean disgust, a hand gesture may mean dismissal, and so on. It is impossible to guess how the patient will interpret one's responses, especially since one is not usually aware of them. Occasionally the patient will ask, "Why do you cross your legs like that?" Although I still don't know what the leg crossing means to him, I now know it means something significant so I explain in some detail why in fact I have crossed my legs: I haven't moved from my chair in a long time, my muscle is cramped, psychiatrists sit for long periods and therefore need to move. I have found that a fairly long, detailed, matter-of-fact explanation calms the patient's misinterpretations. When the patient simply stops talking and stares at me or looks away, I know he or she is reacting to something that I'm not immediately aware of. I then resort to the generalization about it being hard to talk to relative strangers and that new people seem to have strange habits but that as we get accustomed to each other these will become familiar and ordinary. McGlashan (1983), among others, cautions against being overly friendly with a paranoid patient—essentially for the reason that friendliness is prone to misinterpretation. In a distillation of recommendations from other authors, he counsels an initial attitude of distance, coolness, and lack of amusement: "a simple, direct, measured, professional, businesslike demeanor devoid of consuming curiosity" (McGlashan 1983). It is of importance, however, not to playact because an act can only be maintained for so long. It is probably best to be oneself and to know oneself well enough that one can make fairly accurate guesses as to what the patient is reacting to.

By the same token, much can be learned by the patient's nonverbal communication. Even when words do not make sense, the feeling behind the words is usually quite evident, despite the conventional description of the schizophrenic patient showing flatness and inappropriateness. The feelings behind the incomprehensible words, such as rage, anguish, and hopelessness, may be difficult for the therapist to endure so that it is easier to avoid them and to focus instead on trying to decipher words. More therapeutic, however, is to observe and to acknowledge the feelings, to repeatedly make the distinction between feeling something and needing to act on it, to maintain calm despite awareness of stormy feelings, and, progressively, to show the patient how feelings alter perception and can lead to some of the distortions that the patient experiences as symptoms. The patient is not aware of this. Although the patient may acknowledge feelings, he or she perceives them as secondary to perception (someone is following me so I am frightened) rather than primary (I am frightened so I perceive malicious intent in the stranger walking behind me).

Example

Alex was frightened and furious on arrival at his appointment because people on the bus deliberately had pushed against him, had stepped on his feet, and had forced him off at the wrong stop. He stated forcefully that he would no longer be coming to see me because "they" didn't want him to and he had no choice but to obey. The immediate problem was to try to desensitize him from the fear of crowded buses. After he had vented a fair amount of rage and fear, we focused on his mood when he got on the bus. He acknowledged that he was already frustrated because he was afraid of being late, the appointment was at a bad time—the buses were always crowded at that hour—and he felt uncomfortable in crowds. We talked about the initial mood creating an extrasensitivity to pushes and shoves that he otherwise might have ignored. Alex did not totally believe this but did agree that "they" didn't bother him as much at other times of the day when the bus was less crowded. We agreed to change the time of the appointment, devised ways in which he could distract his attention from the crowd (wearing dark glasses and reading a newspaper while on the bus, purchasing a portable headset and listening to music), made another appointment, and, at the end of the session, when he was calmer, reviewed the topic of mood and perception with various pertinent hypothetical examples.

Technical Points

Psychotic Transference

During the course of engaging, it is possible, even probable, for a psychotic transference to develop. In other words, the patient begins to distrust the doctor and to suspect the doctor of hidden motives, of making things worse, of interfering, of hypnotizing him, putting a curse on him, making him fall in love, wiring him up for sound, telling the world his secrets. . . . There are times when these transferences are unmanageable and referral to another therapist is required (Seeman et al. 1982). The delusions usually stem from a perceived hurt (delaying an appointment, making the patient wait, shunning the patient in the hall, seeming to collude with a relative). If left for a time to crystallize and grow without interpretation, the delusions may easily grow to unmanageable dimensions. That is one of the dangers of appointments spaced too far apart. Ideally, if new delusions are permitted expression early and can be clarified and traced to their source, and if alternate explanations can be offered, they will disappear.

Example
Mitch was talking about loneliness and feelings of isolation. I asked about friends and he said he had only one. I inquired about what he and his friend did to combat loneliness and made the seemingly innocuous suggestion that they could occasionally go to the movies since it was lonely to go by oneself. This statement provoked an outburst of rage. Mitch walked out of the office and stated he was not returning. I phoned him later in the day and asked him to come back the next day. He was extremely angry on the phone but agreed to come in order to say goodbye. The next day, still furious, he accused me of making him into a homosexual by encouraging him to have a "date" with his male friend. I was able to refocus on the loneliness, which had made me offer the suggestion and then admitted that I was in error in suggesting how he spend his leisure

time since he, of course, knew better than I what he most enjoyed.

The admission of error is a powerful way of defusing psychotic transference—not error in the sense of having committed the fault one is accused of, but error in something related but peripheral. This is different from what one might do with a nonpsychotic person—that is, point out the distortion and attempt to trace it to childhood origins.

Example
Another example of a potentially unworkable transference reaction is a psychotic erotic transference. Andy, a married schizophrenic man, confronted me with what he perceived was my passion for him. He said I had deliberately phoned when his wife was away (to change an appointment) and had whispered over the phone "I love you." We met several times to straighten this out. I tried the tack of tying in his loneliness during his wife's absence to the resulting misunderstanding of what I had said but he refused to believe this. For a few weeks he phoned me at home, hung up when my husband answered, and sent red roses to the office. His idea was that he would buy two one-way tickets to Rome where we would live happily forever. I am not sure what contributed to the successful resolution of this delusion. I thought of asking for a second opinion, but the delusion was resolved before it was necessary. In fact, I continued to see him and to express interest in him as a person, trying to make the distinction that this was different from seeing him as a potential lover. I also tried as much as possible to be in contact with his wife and asked her to join us in interviews. The alliance survived, perhaps because his marriage was supportive and his wife did not leave him alone often. At any rate, his psychotic thinking subsided rapidly.

Countertransference

Preventing overidentification with patient or family is a problem for many therapists. Being warm and empathic may lead to overinvolvement if there is not some flexibility in the approach and the ability to take distance from the situation as well as to move in closer, as circumstances warrant. Consultation with others helps and discussion with cotherapists can be very helpful, especially when overinvolvement is unrecognized (Seeman et al. 1982).

Dealing With Delusions

An important notion in the engagement phase with a psychotic patient is that truth is many sided and that the patient's view, although many do not believe him or her, is as valid to explore as the alternate meanings that family and friends place on the events in question (Magder 1984). This agreeableness to accept as perhaps true material that is illogical and surreal can make families furious because it gives the therapist's apparent seal of approval to issues that have become contentious at home. Exceptions to the "all is believable" notion are important. If the patient feels that one of the family members or a neighbor is deliberately malevolent, the patient has to be either removed from the situation or disabused of the notion quickly. Otherwise, for patients living at home, this becomes an explosive situation. Sometimes, even in the early stages of the relationship, antipsychotic medication will be accepted as protective against the threat, so that the focus can be on how to stay inwardly strong rather than on measures of counterattack. Alternate explanations for what is happening are accepted best after a therapeutic relationship has developed but even in early stages, many patients will at least *consider* alternate ideas as long as their own are not dealt with dismissively. Possible explanations for the phenomena that the patient experiences are most effectively given tentatively. In other words, doubt is introduced into the certainty of the patient's delusions by a therapist who is experienced as understanding, interested, and intrigued but whose mind is not yet made up (Magder 1984).

There are successful psychiatrists who, in a matter-of-fact way say to their delusional patients, "that's your imagination being overactive," "that's a delusional idea," "that's a product of your illness," and who appear to convince the patient, at least to the extent that the patient returns. Some delusional patients seem to need certainty and will relinquish their own convictions when confronted with a person in authority who gives the strong impression of always being right (Adler 1985).

Talking About the Past

Talking about the past is often considered counterproductive with schizophrenic patients (Munich 1987). It is true that it can be upsetting and regressive for many but, at the same time, there are many patients who remember being relatively trouble free before a certain age and they enjoy talking about "old times." They take pride in early successes and achievements even though the contrast with the present can be sad and sometimes unbearable. I have found that it is worth trying to talk about the past, not in the spirit of inquiry as to what in the past has made the present so hard, but rather about the "good" past, a time of peace and happiness, which then helps to recreate the same sense of peace in the office setting.

Setting

The setting needs to be calming in its own right and free from disturbance as far as is possible. Paradoxically, however, I have often found that being interrupted by an emergency can have a salutary effect on the patient—as if it were a comfort to know that others are also ill, more urgently so in some cases than the patient himself or herself. When I have had to answer the phone in the presence of a schizophrenic patient, almost invariably the patient has paid attention and has been influenced (positively or negatively) by the way I appeared to him or her to have managed the emergency on the phone.

Confidentiality

Whenever others are involved, the issue of confidentiality becomes important. Cotherapists may be individuals who function as semiprofessionals and semifriends. This is often the case with volunteers, activity therapists, and friends or relatives of the patient who are committed to help but who, at the same time, maintain peer rather than therapeutic relations with the patient. How much does one tell about the patient? Certain information may be vital but cannot be divulged if it was told in confidence. There is no easy answer to this. I try, wherever possible, to hold joint meetings and to hope that the necessary information will come spontaneously from the patient during those times. Joint meetings also serve the purpose of aligning everyone (patient, family, therapists) on the same side so that they are not seen as opponents or antagonists in the patient's mind. On some occasions, it may be necessary to exclude some potential helpers—for example, family members—because the patient refuses to have anything to do with them and will have nothing to do with the doctor unless he or she also shuns the family. In those instances, in order to cement the relationship, the doctor has little choice but to explain to the relative that there can be no communication between them. When the relationship with the patient solidifies, there may be a profound change in the unforgiving stance taken against the family.

As subsequent chapters will show, attitudes, expectations, and technical strategies change over time in the course of long-term association with the individual. All three parties—patient, therapist, and family—become knowledgeable about each other and much of the initial suspiciousness and difficulty slowly disappear. The initial phase is crucial, however, because the future of treatment and the future for that patient depend on the doctor's ability to engage the patient in the lifelong work of developing and maintaining relationships.

References

Adler DA: A framework for the analysis of psychotherapeutic approaches to schizophrenia. Yale J Biol Med 58:219–225, 1985

Anonymous: "Can we talk?" The schizophrenic patient in psychotherapy. Am J Psychiatry 143:68–70, 1986

Camenietzki S, Albott W: How to fail in the treatment of schizophrenic people. Bull Menninger Clin 40:118–124, 1976

Docherty JP, Fiester SJ: The therapeutic alliance and compliance with psychopharmacology, in Psychiatry Update: American Psychiatric Association Annual Review, Vol 4. Edited by Hales RE, Frances AJ. Washington, DC, American Psychiatric Press, 1985, pp 607–632

Greben SE: The essence of psychotherapy. Br J Psychiatry 138:449–455, 1981

Greben SE: Psychotherapy today: further consideration of the essence of psychotherapy. Br J Psychiatry 151:283–287, 1987

Keats CJ, McGlashan TH: Intensive psychotherapy of schizophrenia. Yale J Biol Med 58:239–254, 1985

Magder D: Seeing the person behind the psychosis. Canadian Family Physician 30:369–372, 1984

McGlashan TH: DSM-III schizophrenia and individual psychotherapy. J Nerv Ment Dis 170:752–757, 1982

McGlashan TH: Intensive individual psychotherapy of schizophrenia: a review of techniques. Arch Gen Psychiatry 40:909–920, 1983

Munich RL: Conceptual trends and issues in the psychotherapy of schizophrenia. Am J Psychother 41:23–37, 1987

Searles HF: The schizophrenic individual's experience of his world. Psychiatry 30:119–131, 1967

Seeman MV, Pyke J, Denberg D, et al: Co-therapy in a schizophrenia clinic. Can J Psychiatry 27:296–300, 1982

Strupp HH: Toward a specification of teaching and learning in psychotherapy. Arch Gen Psychiatry 21:203–212, 1969

Tuma AH, May PRA, Yale C, et al: Therapist characteristics and the outcome of treatment in schizophrenia. Arch Gen Psychiatry 35:81–85, 1978

Werman DS: Technical aspects of supportive psychotherapy. Psychiatr J Univ Ottawa 5:153–160, 1981

Chapter 4

Individual Psychotherapy

STANLEY E. GREBEN, M.D., F.R.C.P.(C)

Chapter 4

Individual Psychotherapy

*I*ndividual psychotherapy with patients who have schizophrenia can take as many forms as does individual psychotherapy with patients who have other disorders. As much potential exists for positive therapeutic results as is the case with neurotic disorders or disorders of character. The diagnosis of schizophrenia does not in itself dictate the form or the duration of the psychotherapy. These are more determined by the patient's interest in and motivation toward psychotherapeutic help as well as, of course, by the resources available. Most important, a diagnosis of schizophrenia does not indicate that psychotherapy should be superficial and supportive, because, modified to take into account the severity of the patient's illness, it is often the case that success in psychotherapy can be achieved, and significant change in the patient can be effected, given time.

Sigmund Freud felt that because the cause of the major psychoses would likely turn out to be biological, and because of the nature of schizophrenic symptoms, psychoanalysis would not be helpful for patients with schizophrenia (Freud 1925). It is true that the use of unmodified classical psychoanalysis is inappropriate with this disorder. It is not true, as some subsequently concluded, that insight-oriented, psychodynamically based psychotherapies are contraindicated. In fact, long experience has demonstrated that schizophrenic patients not only deserve but require individual psychotherapy in order to make significant, even impressive therapeutic gains.

The use of individual psychotherapy in no way precludes

the use of other forms of treatment. Group psychotherapy, family psychotherapy, and psychopharmacologic agents are discussed in other chapters, but this is not to suggest that each of these should be used alone. The best approach to an individual schizophrenic patient is one that considers the possible concomitant or consecutive use of various of these treatments. Nothing about the judicious, appropriate use of other forms of treatment should interfere with the efficacy of individual psychotherapy.

Some of those who first used intensive psychotherapy with patients with schizophrenia are referred to in Chapter 1. The work of Sullivan and Fromm-Reichmann led to a psychotherapeutic approach to such patients at Chestnut Lodge in Rockville, Maryland. Others such as Otto Will (1971) and Lewis Hill (1957) taught and wrote helpfully with regard to this work. Hannah Green recorded in moving fictional form her experience as a patient of Fromm-Reichmann in *I Never Promised You a Rose Garden* (Green 1964).

Therapeutic Elements of Individual Psychotherapy

Psychotherapy with all patients has two principal elements that can be therapeutically effective (Greben 1987). The first is understanding or insight that emerges from the talking and listening that takes place between the therapist and the patient. The second is the relationship itself that exists between the two individuals. These two elements are closely linked, and each contributes to the other. Examining together the patient's history, feelings, and behavior puts the patient and therapist into a working alliance, which is the second important facet of their relationship. The first is, of course, a personal relationship, since they come as two individual people, bringing to the work their own personal characteristics and backgrounds. As they work together, some of the ways in which they respond to each other are strongly influenced by conflictual feelings that arise out of their own past lives, and these feelings, called *transference* on the part of the patient, and *countertransference* on the part of the therapist, compose the third facet of their relationship. It is the scrutiny and understanding of the most intensive parts of those transference feelings that can be most influential in ultimately bringing about psychological changes in the patient.

Whereas each of these two basic elements of the psychotherapeutic encounter is important in all psychotherapy, in the work with schizophrenic patients the aspects that have to do with the relationship between patient and therapist are of cardinal significance. The greatest attention must be given, from the outset, to the need to slowly establish a bond between the two participants. This must take place slowly in most instances, because the patient is so afraid of being hurt in any of a variety of ways. None of these ways is unique to patients with schizophrenia, for all of them are ways in which we are all afraid of being emotionally hurt. In schizophrenic patients, however, these fears are magnified, because such people have been so injured, so often, by so many others.

To review, then, what I have said: as in all individual psychotherapy, working with patients with schizophrenia involves three portions of the combination of patient and psychotherapist—the personal relationship, the working alliance, and the transference and countertransference aspects of the relationship. The greatest change can come about when it is possible for the two people working together to examine and discuss the past, the present, and the various aspects of the therapeutic relationship. With patients who have schizophrenia, it is almost always necessary to use more than one form of treatment, and it is always important to provide some elements of individual psychotherapy.

Special Characteristics of Individual Psychotherapy With Schizophrenic Patients

I have stated previously that psychotherapy with schizophrenic patients is not basically different from such work with patients with other disorders. However, there are characteristics of schizophrenia to which the psychiatrist must be especially sensitive in approaching such patients psychotherapeutically.

The first aspect of psychotherapeutic treatment of patients with schizophrenia has to do with the fact that the symptoms of the illness have themselves such a profound effect upon the person, his life, and those around him. This means that the first matter to be dealt with are those symptoms, for they are so absorbing, distracting, worrisome, and frightening that they rob the patient of much of the mental energy that will ultimately be required to engage in the psychotherapy. Thus psychosocial and pharmacologic interventions pave the way for psychotherapeutic ones; for example, when the interventions relieve the patient of enervating symptoms, they allow him or her to engage more freely in the work of the psychotherapy.

It is essential to proceed slowly and carefully, for hurting or frightening such patients can be irretrievably damaging to the prospect of being able to work together. I have referred to this earlier, and the point cannot be overstated. It does not mean that such patients have to be handled as though they were made of fragile china, for that would feel artificial and not genuine to the patient. It does mean that even greater than usual attention to being tactful, thoughtful, and open is indicated.

Since there are always other practical matters to be dealt with, these can be the focus of attention in the early period of working together. Hospital admission and later discharge may be required. The use of some medications will ordinarily be necessary, at least for a time. This often requires discussion of which medications, in what dose, and in what combinations. Practical issues related to family, friends, home, school, or work will need to be discussed. It may seem that all these matters are extraneous to the psychotherapy, but that is not the case, for while they are being attended to, the patient is becoming more familiar with the therapist and learning to what extent it is safe to deal with him or her.

It is an artificial distinction to consider that dealing with practical, external matters is one thing, and that the personal examination of the individual who is in psychotherapy is another. In fact, both are important portions of the psychotherapy itself, for dealing with practical matters achieves two goals: the first is that the patient is helped to solve external problems that are troubling him or her; the second is that in the process of doing so, the therapeutic relationship is allowed to grow. When one works with a patient with schizophrenia, one is constantly being examined and measured by the patient, both consciously and unconsciously. It might be said that in the early phases of such treatment the therapist is being accepted "on approval" only, and that whether or not the combination of the two people involved can survive will remain to be determined by the patient's reaction to how he or she finds the therapist to be. The therapist will become known through how he or she behaves, and will be assessed by the patient through what he or she says and does. There can be no substitute for the therapist's allowing himself or herself to be examined and appraised directly by the patient.

The patient with schizophrenia has good reason to be mistrustful of others. First, the patient has had repeated disappointments in others who have found him or her to be difficult to be with, or who have found it too much to continue to put up with his or her problems. Second, the schizophrenic patient has had to carry the burden of the symptoms of the illness, and this has left him or her too little energy to deal with others in comfortable ways. Third, the patient is not usual or average, but is rather different or strange, and this has made many people deal with him or her with excessive care. Fourth, the patient has had little experience of people who persist in their interest in him or her and continue to relate warmly and positively to him or her. Fifth, the patient may have paranoid ideas that magnify his or her basic suspiciousness of people, and may have auditory hallucinations or delusional ideas that tell the patient that his or her welfare cannot be entrusted to others. All of these factors contribute to a great doubt on the part of the patient that he or she will ever find someone whose caring and interest can be relied upon.

None of what I have just described resides exclusively in those who are schizophrenic, for this is the substance of a principal human dilemma: how to find people with whom one can establish close, warm, and reciprocal relationships, avoiding the hurt of either abandonment or abuse. All people struggle with the wish to be close to others and, at the same time, the fear of the danger of such closeness. In people who have schizophrenia, this struggle is magnified, for the person feels extremely vulnerable to hurt, and has to live with the memory of repeated instances of having been deeply injured by others.

All of this places a great potential strain upon the therapeutic relationship, one that could not possibly be resolved quickly. It means that of necessity the process of learning to trust the therapist will be a slow one. It is not months but years that will be required for the fearful distrust that resides in the patient to gradually diminish.

Very often patients with schizophrenia have become terribly entangled in their relationships with family members. Some have felt that those entanglements have probably been causative of schizophrenia, but most people today do not believe this. Rather, it is the other way about: the burdens on and within the patient make for frustrating relationships with others, and those closest to the patient, especially parents and perhaps siblings, get caught in complex webs that are discouraging and defeating to all concerned.

When working with such patients, the therapist often finds that such entanglements may very well develop in the therapeutic relationship, and this is something that, not surprisingly, the patient also anticipates and fears. This means that the therapist will be challenged to achieve an appropriate closeness to, and yet sufficient distance from the patient. Sometimes it will be difficult to discern the boundary lines between patient and therapist, and this can be worrisome to the patient and frustrating to the therapist. The patient needs to depend upon the therapist, yet not to such a degree that he or she feels the same sense of being smothered that he or she has already experienced with some others. The therapist wants to have sufficient closeness to the patient to be able to feel he or she knows the patient, but not to such a degree that he or she feels bogged down in the world of the patient's fears and misconceptions.

All of this is to say that in working with a patient with schizophrenia the matter of closeness or distance will always be a challenge and that the therapist will repeatedly be called upon to be close enough to understand and to nourish the patient emotionally, and yet distant enough to retain objectivity and to permit the patient to function, increasingly, as a separate, discrete individual.

These various aspects that make working with schizophrenic patients in psychotherapy demanding for the therapist have led many practitioners to the false conclusion that such work is neither fruitful nor worthwhile. Indeed, despite the special circumstances that must be borne in mind in such work, experience has shown that persisting in such endeavors can be highly productive for both patient and psychiatrist.

The idea that patients with schizophrenia neither want nor can benefit from psychotherapy is based upon a fantasy that, while understandable, is far from reality. Because such patients seem strange to others, it is easy to think that they have neither the emotional needs nor the emotional capacities that most people have. Whereas it is true that some such patients, having been abused or neglected for many years, cannot find their way to the normal expression of emotions to other people, it is a minority of these patients who are in that position, and the majority will, in time, be emotionally available to a therapist who is sufficiently persistent and sensitive. If one accepts the schizophrenic patient's defenses at face value, then one will draw the misguided impression that he or she is blunted and distant, perhaps uncaring about the world around him or her. If one is not convinced by the protective symptoms, one may in time be offered access to the patient's rich inner life—fears, anxieties, sadness, doubts, wishes, and satisfactions. In the face of manifest differences observed in others, it is easy to comfort ourselves with the opinion that they are different from us in kind, rather than in degree, and that it is useless and unnecessary to try to reach through to them. If, on the other hand, we start with the conviction that their strangeness is in large part defensive, and that their inner lives are different from ours very largely in degree only, then we may be offered, eventually, the opportunity to enter their worlds.

In an article entitled "Can We Talk?"—The Schizophrenic Patient in Psychotherapy" (Anonymous 1986), a patient expresses clearly the importance that psychotherapeutic work has had in the process of recovering from this illness.

> Even if one adheres to the belief that psychotherapy lends itself more to emotionally oriented problems than to something which appears to be more biochemical, one must take into consideration the emotional aspects of schizophrenia. Besides the day-to-day stress of contending with what often seems to be a monster raging inside one's mind, there are emotional problems that have evolved and accumulated over the course of the patient's life. . . .
>
> I was once told that I had a very strong observing ego, and I was fascinated and encouraged to think of my mind having that power to step away from the craziness, to look at it and understand it. Perhaps that is why therapy has worked so well for me—this capacity and a strong motivation to develop it have driven me to uncover what it is about my mind that makes me retreat into craziness when the stresses of my life, real or imagined, become unbearable. . . . I had drawn so far inside myself and so far away from the world, I had to be shown not only that the world was safe but also that I belonged to it, that I was in fact a person. . . .
>
> The question of whether the fragile ego of the schizophrenic patient can withstand the rigors of intensive therapy seems to me an unfortunate hindrance to the willingness of psychiatrists to attempt psychotherapy with schizophrenic individuals. A fragile ego left alone remains fragile. It seems there must be some balance that can be achieved so that schizophrenic patients can receive the benefits of psychotherapy with therapists who are sensitive to their special needs and can help their egos emerge, little by little. Medication or superficial support alone is not a substitute for the feeling that one is understood by another human being.

These comments bring out clearly how appropriate individual psychotherapy can be of unique value with schizophrenic patients, when suitably employed. They also indicate that the therapeutic work involves special challenges that demand a great deal from both patient and therapist, but which do not in any way render the therapy inadvisable. On the contrary, such difficult and demanding work can be highly productive. The most important message in this patient's sensitive and insightful observations is that through individual psychotherapy something was achieved that took the patient further than it was possible to go with the use of other forms of treatment. It is essential to understand that for such patients the best end result is likely when a variety of modes of treatment are employed, but that the use of other forms of treatment does not obviate the need for individual psychotherapy. It is also important to know that such patients should not be restricted to only superficial and supportive psychotherapy, for it is entirely possible to use deeper, insight-oriented treatment when it is employed in ways that are sensitive to the special needs and vulnerabilities of the patients.

Example
Martha was raised in a highly successful, educated family. She was always known to be very sensitive and shy, though her family connections brought her, in childhood and young adulthood, in contact with many good people. In her early twenties she became progressively more depressed and withdrawn, and finally became psychotic in a markedly paranoid way. She was admitted to a psychiatric hospital, where she was helped to come out of the acute psychotic state through the use of major antipsychotic medication as well as, for a shorter time, a tricyclic antidepressant.

I had met Martha briefly during her most disturbed period and encouraged and helped arrange her admission to hospital. After her discharge, she began to visit me as an outpatient, while continuing with antipsychotic medication. From that time until the present, two decades later, she and I have continued a psychotherapeutic relationship.

In the early days of our work together it was very difficult to talk with Martha, because she was so shy and suspicious. She did not believe at that time that admission to the hospital had been either necessary or helpful. Indeed, she continued to have paranoid delusions about the ill intentions of some of the people she knew and felt that a plot existed against her. In the beginning she was highly suspicious of me, not so much in that I wanted, as the others did, to harm her, but rather that I knew very well what they were up to and was lying to protect them and to deceive her.

It gradually emerged that behind the intimidated blushing exterior of this attractive young woman lay a great pressure of powerful feelings—sadness, rage, envy, and fear. Many times, once she had begun to get over her fear of me, she would berate me, accusing me of deception and dishonesty. That she was increasingly able to openly express such negative feelings toward me was a great achievement for her. Though I often wondered whether there was enough of a bond in our relationship to have her continue to come to our sessions, she did in fact persevere. Gradually, over the early years when we met for an hour once a week, she came to feel that it was safe to let me know what she was feeling and experiencing. As this continued, she became increasingly able to function in the outside world. She managed to obtain work, which in the beginning was somewhat more than she could handle, for it involved working all day long with other people, and she was convinced that most of them thought her strange and discussed her and were contemptuous of her. When I challenged these ideas of reference she always insisted that either I did not understand her plight or else I purposely chose to deceive her. Nonetheless, the paranoid ideas gradually diminished in intensity over months and years, so that eventually they only returned when she felt herself to be under particular stress.

As the years passed, we gradually decreased the frequency of her visits, first to every second week, then every month, then every 2 months. At present we do not have prearranged appointments, but she calls to see me when she feels the need; she usually comes a few times a year. Sometimes she manages well with no medication, occasionally she will take a small daily dose of neuroleptic. She has held the same job for many years now and is highly responsible. Although she fears the opposite, she is clearly a valued employee. She travels widely on holidays, sometimes alone, sometimes with a relative or friend. Over the years she has developed satisfying, close relationships with a number of people, though at times she still fears that she cannot have normal, adequate relations with others. Martha continues to talk, when she is worried and under stress, as though I am not trusted or believed by her, yet she functions as though what I say to her is of considerable importance. Whenever we have discussed our working together she will mobilize a grudging agreement that it likely has been of help, but she is made very uncomfortable with such discussion. She hesitatingly admits that she is functioning much better than could have been predicted years ago when she was so floridly ill. In fact she manages very well and has become a great deal more self-possessed than I would have anticipated when we first met.

Although we see each other quite infrequently, she understands that I am available to her, but that there is no need to come when she feels well. When things pile up and distress her, she will come, and as soon as she enters my office she immediately plunges into what she has been thinking and feeling, as though we had met not long before. The working relationship continues in her mind and feelings, even when we do not see each other for a period of months.

It was an act of great trust, to her a dangerous act, for Martha to open herself to my view. She was terribly afraid of expressing many of the things that she felt, but she was forced to do so because of the desperate emotional plight in which she found herself. She required a human contact that in the end proved to be safe for her, in order to make her way back into the world of other people. She achieved a great deal and this has allowed her to lead a life that, although often painful, would be seen as normal by most observers. What is even more important, she herself now takes considerable satisfaction, even pleasure, in living.

The Psychotherapeutic Relationship

In all individual psychotherapy, two essential portions can be recognized. The first is the content, the second the context.

By the *content* I mean the material that the patient brings to the psychotherapeutic discussion: thoughts, feelings, ideas, memories, and dreams. These will be examined and discussed and, where possible, understood. The explanations made by the psychotherapist may be more superficial and conscious (clarifications), or deeper and more unconscious (interpretations). In both instances the patient is strengthened through understanding (insight). Thus, dealing with content is of great importance, but must not overshadow the significance of the other highly valuable portion of the therapy: the context. By *context* I mean the circumstances in which the therapy takes place: the arrangements between the two parties, the physical setting in which they meet, and their relationship itself. Of these, the most vital is the relationship that is developed between patient and therapist. In order to understand the relationship more clearly, it is best to divide it into three parts. Two real people meet together, so there is a *real relationship.* They begin to work together, so there develops a *therapeutic or working alliance.* In the course of that work distortions occur because of the emotional histories of both the parties, so there is a *transference relationship,* in which incompletely resolved early conflicts cause magnified or distorted feelings in the patient (transference) and in the therapist (countertransference). These three portions of the therapeutic relationship are important in all psychotherapy, including in the therapy of patients with schizophrenia.

The three portions of the therapeutic relationship help the patient in different ways. Having a real relationship with someone who will be available over a long period, likely years, is a highly important experience for the schizophrenic patient. All people fear abuse or abandonment at the hands of other people, and such fears are very great in those who have schizophrenia. Such people have been hurt, ignored, and often abandoned by people, and they consequently expect abuse or neglect at the hands of all others, including the therapist. When a long-standing relationship between schizophrenic patient and therapist occurs without serious misuse or avoidance of the patient, the patient will be profoundly affected, and a kind of healing or growth occurs within the patient. Most often such patients have not had the advantage of good real relationships with others, so that if the therapist succeeds in establishing and maintaining such a relationship with the patient, this can have a most salubrious effect upon the patient.

While examining the real relationship between patient and therapist it is important to point out that the relationship must have certain characteristics if it is to succeed. All patients prefer that their psychotherapists be genuine, honest, down-to-earth, authentic, unpretentious, and (as far as possible) natural. Unfortunately, psychiatrists, through their training and because of a misunderstanding of Freud's injunction to remain objective and like a mirror or surgeon, have often become unresponsive in ways that interfere with psychotherapy (Greben 1981). With schizophrenic patients it is even more vitally important than with less ill patients that the therapist not indulge in such artificial modes of behavior, for such patients are especially sensitive to excessive distance or coolness on the part of others. Hence, in the real relationship with the schizophrenic patient the therapist must be available, visible, and in emotional contact with the patient. There should be no effort on the part of the therapist to distance or hide himself or herself from the patient, for the patient will, understandably, experience this as rejection by the therapist or as an attitude of condescending superiority on the part of the therapist. Real people need to be treated by real people, and with schizophrenic patients this is even more pointedly so. Thus, in the real relationship with the patient the therapist must be perceived as concerned, warm, humane, and involved.

In the therapeutic or working alliance with the schizophrenic patient the psychotherapist must be engaged in a cooperative, mutual task with someone he or she treats as humanly equal. Of course the patient is troubled and disadvantaged, and the therapist is educated and trained to do the work and experienced in the doing of it, so the therapist is, relatively speaking, advantaged. At the same time the therapist is not ill or imbalanced and presumably has his or her life under a reasonable degree of control. Nonetheless, the working alliance must be felt by the patient to be a partnership to which both participants bring their capacities and wish to succeed.

The mutuality of such an arrangement will be at first surprising but later most satisfying to the patient.

Most patients who are schizophrenic have had few if any cooperative relationships in which they have, together with another person, worked long and diligently toward a shared goal. One of the most satisfying aspects of psychotherapy for such a person can be the unusual opportunity to be taken seriously while cooperatively engaged in a serious shared enterprise. There can be not just satisfaction but actual growth that arises out of the successful pursuit of such a long-standing undertaking.

Dealing with the transference and countertransference aspects of the therapeutic relationship is of the utmost importance in the therapeutic work with schizophrenic patients, and this occurs in two ways. The first is experiential, whereby the patient has the pleasant surprise that the negative experiences he or she had expected do not occur. Let us say that the patient has, as had my patient Martha, the expectation of being treated badly, even plotted against maliciously by all people, including the therapist. This is a transference expectation based on beliefs that were developed earlier in the patient's life and have persisted so as to apply to all people. When the patient has a better experience than was expected in the therapeutic relationship, and when this happens against expectations again and again over the years, then something changes in the patient. Many writers have explained this therapeutic phenomenon in different ways, but one of the simplest and clearest was that of Franz Alexander, who called it a "corrective emotional experience" (Alexander 1956). Identifying the experiential factor in this way does not of course explain exactly how it works, but experienced psychotherapists have ample evidence that it does work. With patients who are schizophrenic, this experiential therapeutic effect that can gradually alter transference distortions is of the greatest significance.

The second way in which transference issues significantly affect such patients occurs when the therapist can discuss with and explain to the patient the evidence for and origins of transference distortions that occur between them. When such matters as, for example, angry outbursts against the therapist, strong fears toward him or her, or loving and erotic attractions to him or her can be discussed by the two participants, then a fuller, further degree of change can come about than can arise in any other way. In part this is because of the development of insight, to which I have referred above. In part it is because of tremendous relief that the schizophrenic patient will feel to know that the morass of feelings in which he or she has always felt immersed can be sorted out, identified, and accepted. Until this happens, such patients ordinarily feel strange, bizarre, and unnatural. When their feelings can be identified and named by simple everyday words, they feel less strange and more human. The therapist will, implicitly and explicitly, be saying to the patient that whereas the patient is a unique human being, all of the thoughts and feelings that he or she has had are experienced by all other human beings even, by implication, by the therapist. This is most important for the patient to understand, for so often such patients feel so alien that they take themselves to be entirely different creatures from all the other people who inhabit the earth. Identifying, labeling, and discovering the personal, historical origins of the transference distortions can be most helpful to the patient, allowing him or her to feel human, rather than inhuman; normal, rather than abnormal; and acceptable, rather than repulsive.

I must point out here that the degree to which transference distortions can be identified and discussed with schizophrenic patients varies a good deal from patient to patient. With many patients, after months or years of work, it becomes comfortable and easy to discuss such issues. With others it does not become possible, as the patient needs to be allowed to be at arm's length from the therapist and discussing feelings of such immediacy to both parties remains too threatening to the patient. With every schizophrenic patient, then, the therapist will need to determine the extent to which such scrutiny of transference feelings is possible. One cannot make such a decision in advance. Rather, the therapist will have to find or feel his or her way to that furthest point of transference exploration that is possible with any given schizophrenic patient.

As for countertransference feelings, here again the extent to which they can be discussed with a given patient will have to be determined by the therapist within the clinical context. All patients tend to make the therapist into someone who is essentially unlike themselves, and that includes the view that the therapist does not have feelings like those that the patient has. Patients with schizophrenia have such misapprehensions even more strongly than the average general patient so that, when it is possible for the patient to come to know the human feelings, including distortions, on the part of the therapist, this can often be most helpful to the patient. An error on the part of the therapist, an angry response when one needn't have occurred, or other evidence of the therapist's deeper emotional conflicts may in some ways be upsetting to the patient but may in more ways be comforting to him or her. Patients tend to idealize their therapists, just in the same way that children tend to idealize their parents. Patients with schizophrenia feel like underdeveloped, unworthy children and see their therapists as almost-perfect giants. When therapists make the mistake of encouraging or fostering such idealizations, the patient feels worse and worse, like an unworthy supplicant at the feet of the wonderful therapist. When the patient is allowed, even helped to see the therapist for what he or she presumably is—a decent, hardworking professional who has personal limitations as well as strengths—then the patient will feel better about both himself or herself and the therapist. This recognition of the therapist's human frailties and conflicts, as well as assets and capacities, can be most liberating to the patient with schizophrenia, for it can win him or her a place, along with the therapist, in the real, ordinary world of real and ordinary people. Gaining entry, in the patient's own mind, to that world, is an enormous achievement on the parts of both the schizophrenic patient and the therapist who wishes to be of help to such a patient.

The work of individual psychotherapy with any patient is

not dramatic and moving most of the time. Rather, it involves patient and persistent pursuit of the freedom that can come from understanding, honesty, integrity, and a reasonable working relationship between two mutually respectful, caring human beings. With those who are afflicted with the disorder that we call schizophrenia, this is also the case. Individual psychotherapy involves the dogged tasks of meeting together, seeking understanding, learning to recognize and to tolerate emotional pain, and, most important, not giving up. The resurrection of hope that comes from the work of psychotherapy is of essential importance (Frank 1968). With schizophrenic patients it is the central core of the psychotherapeutic work and can make available to the patient a life that is three- rather than two-dimensional.

Individual psychotherapy over an extended period can hold out to the patient with schizophrenia the promise of a place in the world that others inhabit, so that he or she no longer feels as alien or alone. This part of the treatment of schizophrenia can only be achieved in one way: through real, authentic interaction with another interested, humane, and able human being. It is a dimension of the greatest significance in the treatment of patients with schizophrenia.

References

Alexander F: Psychoanalysis and Psychotherapy. New York, WW Norton, 1956

Anonymous: "Can we talk?"—the schizophrenic patient in psychotherapy. Am J Psychiatry 143:68–70, 1986

Frank JD: The role of hope in psychotherapy. Int J Psychiatry 5:383–395, 1968

Freud S: An autobiographical study (1925), in The Standard Edition of the Complete Psychological Works of Sigmund Freud, Vol XX. Translated and edited by Strachey J. London, Hogarth Press, 1959, pp 7–74

Greben SE: Unresponsiveness: the demon artefact of psychotherapy. Am J Psychother 35:244–250, 1981

Greben SE: Psychotherapy today: further consideration of the essence of psychotherapy. Br J Psychiatry 151:283–287, 1987

Green H: I Never Promised You a Rose Garden. New York, Holt, Reinhart, & Winston, 1964

Hill LB: Psychotherapy of a schizophrenic. Am J Psychoanal 17:99–109, 1957

Will OA: Psychotherapy and schizophrenia: implications for human living. Proceedings of the IV International Symposium on Psychotherapy of Schizophrenia. Amsterdam, Excerpta Medica, 1971, pp 25–37

Chapter 5

Family Therapy

LEOPOLDO CHAGOYA, M.D., F.R.C.P.(C)

Chapter 5

Family Therapy

When the genetic origin of schizophrenia became more generally accepted (Gottesman and Shields 1982), statements such as the following began appearing in the psychiatric literature: "Now we can dispense with the psychodynamic theories that blame the family for schizophrenic pathology."

The thorough clinician has to appreciate not only the value of the biological evidence of organic pathology in schizophrenia, but also the psychosocial dimension of the pathological process. The family plays an important role in the control of the illness, in the prevention of relapses, and in the success of the ongoing treatment of schizophrenic patients.

Early Theories

In the late 1950s, Lidz et al. (1957) advanced the first of a series of theories in which the environment of the schizophrenic patient was seen as the predominating factor that unchained the psychosis. Clinicians observed that the hospitalized schizophrenic patient frequently relapsed on weekends spent at home. This set the clinical staff of hospitals wondering what there was in the familial environment that promoted the psychosis. Complete families were hospitalized, and the interaction of family members and the schizophrenic patient was observed. At this time, attention was focused on the effects of the family on the schizophrenic patient; the effects of the schizophrenic patient on the family was ignored.

Bateson, with a group of keen observers of family interaction, developed the theory of the "double bind" (Bateson et al. 1956). This term refers to a specific type of repetitive interaction between a mothering person and her schizophrenic son or daughter. It encompasses the following components: 1) a negative injunction ("Don't do X"); 2) a positive injunction that contradicts the other, expressed verbally or nonverbally ("Do X"); 3) a prohibition in which the "victim" of such contradictory messages is forbidden to see the contradiction or comment on it: this is done not in an open manner but by innuendo and in nonverbal ways; and 4) a prohibition in which the "victim" is not allowed to escape the field.

This situation takes place when the schizophrenic patient and the double-binder are very close and grow to believe that their togetherness has survival value. They establish thus what is called a *symbiotic relationship*. The clinician can test this: suggested separation of the two members of a symbiotic dyad will meet intense resistance from each member of the pair, both fearing that some catastrophe will take place if separation occurs.

The double-bind produces in the "victim" a feeling of always being wrong, a feeling of "damned if I do and damned if I don't," anxiety about incurring the parent's disapproval, and anger at being treated in such an incomprehensible manner. As a consequence, some authors believed that the double bind was the main schizophrenogenic factor that unleashed the psychotic symptoms. Therapeutic attempts at dealing with double-binding parents were only at times successful.

As part of environmentalism, some articles documented how the family transmission of thought disorder resulted in schizophrenic symptoms (Lidz et al. 1958) and described disorders in family communication that included inconsistencies, contradictions, non sequiturs, and loose ends.

Another useful theory in understanding the role of the schizophrenic patient in the family had to do with the phenomenon of scapegoating (Ackerman 1958). The premise was that when the couple in conflict has trouble facing marital differences and tensions, it will unconsciously turn toward one child, label him or her as "the bad one," and interpret all of the child's actions as responsible for the family distress. Phrases like "If it wasn't for Johnnie, this family would be happy" exemplify this basic family attitude. The schizophrenic family member, thus, was not seen as ill or deviant, but as a victim of his or her family. Even though the literature was filled with admonitions against making the family feel guilty, an unforeseen result of environmentalist thinking was that the clinicians treating families harbored a subliminal resentment against the family for having harmed the schizophrenic patient. These theories promoted a type of therapy that increased guilt and "expressed emotion" (criticism and intrusiveness) in the families.

Early Therapies

In the 1960s, the objectives of family therapy were: 1) to clarify the communication within the family on many levels; 2) to improve the emotional contact among family members; 3) to encourage family members to express inhibited feelings; and 4) to try to liberate the patient from a victim or scapegoat position, de-emphasizing his or her sick or deviant role (Ackerman 1966; Lidz et al. 1957; Singer and Wynne 1965).

As time went on, families found that, during therapy sessions, they were expected to present only problems or negative experiences. The origins of these were then traced to the parents' failure to be clear or empathic or to promote autonomy in their children. Even though the analyses of such interactions were *accurate,* families came out of the sessions feeling sad, depressed, guilty, and unwilling to return. They did not feel that the therapist was their ally; they felt that he or she was working to favor the schizophrenic patient at the expense of the family. This experience of family members is poignantly described in the book *Families Helping Families* (Dearth et al. 1986).

Family Groups

Families started joining others to share information and practical hints on how to deal with a schizophrenic family member. Laqueur et al. (1964) were among the first psychiatrists to encourage families of schizophrenic individuals to share with each other, in a group, the practicalities of how to handle the crises of living with a schizophrenic family member as a son, as a daughter, as a sibling, or as a parent. Atwood and Williams (1978) documented the value of group support for these families, with emphasis on education, sharing experiences, and self-help. Family treatment sessions acquired a pace slower than that of previous family therapies. The relatives found value in understanding the illness, the medications, and the best ways of responding to schizophrenic symptoms at home. They began to see the difficulties psychiatric staff encountered in treating the illness, so, rather than attacking doctors, they became allies by collaborating with the treating team for the welfare of the schizophrenic patient. At the same time, the medical staff, rather than blaming and criticizing, developed partisanship with the patient's relatives. Sets of parents also met without their schizophrenic offspring to offer each other social support, which turned out to be very important in the management of the schizophrenic offspring. Parents groups focused also on working through their own guilt and disappointment in order to become more independent from the patient. Many times the patient had been allowed to be a tyrant who ruled the family with his or her symptoms and "imprisoned" the relatives as copatients in the household or in the hospital. Common themes in groups of parents and relatives of schizophrenic persons include how to socialize without the patient, how to reduce guilt and isolation, how to reduce fear of relinquishing control, how to accept the degree of the patient's handicap, and how to diminish the schizophrenic patient's power over the family without increasing the level of expressed emotion. Psychiatrists now hold crisis-oriented individual meetings when necessary. The mistakes the family makes in the way they deal with their schizophrenic member are seen as a lack of skills they need to learn. In this way, meetings with the family therapist become a supportive, emotionally controlled, and gratifying experience.

Example

Mrs. F has been in individual psychotherapy with me for over a year. Session after session she elaborates on how difficult it is for her to carry on her life knowing her son is in a chronic psychiatric ward, at times hallucinating, unable to eat well, unable to take care of himself, surrounded by other psychotics. She is a widow who lives with her daughter, a successful lawyer. She could have a pleasant and productive life. However, her sense of guilt, her feeling of responsibility, her doubts about whether she is doing enough for her son, and her search for the answer to her son's illness cause her to spend many days and nights "imprisoned" (her word) with him in that ward. At the beginning of her treatment with me, she visited her son every day, allowed abuse and insults from him, tried to follow the flow of his psychotic thought disorder, and repeatedly suggested to doctors and nurses better ways of treating her son. In her eyes, her suggestions would lead to improved results. The hospital staff, however, saw her as a nuisance and as an overprotective mother. Through the course of her own treatment, Mrs. F has been able to accept the limits of what she can do to "save her son from schizophrenia." Again and again she has decided to set limits and not allow him to seduce her into psychotic communication. Again and again she does not implement her decisions. She periodically relapses and becomes—in her own words—"another crazy person." Mrs. F combines a propensity to allow herself to be mistreated (to atone for the guilt she feels) with an omnipotent belief that she will find a way the doctors have not found to cure her son. Only when she solves her exaggerated sense of responsibility and gives up her dreams of being the one who saves her son will she become freer to carry on with her life.

Newer Theories and Therapies

In the mid-1970s, Brown et al. (1972) and Vaughn and Leff (1976) established that a high level of "expressed emotion" (EE factor, defined as hostility, criticism, and intrusiveness) un-chains the psychotic process in the schizophrenic patient. In view of such evidence, therapeutic efforts aim now at lowering expressed emotion and improving the social isolation between the family and the outside world. The clinician explores thoroughly the ideology of the family, since not every family professes the same values nor shares identical attitudes toward a schizophrenic family member. The clinician meets the family at their level, especially at times of crisis (Langsley et al. 1968). In Chapter 3, Seeman points out how valuable it is to surrender the role of the expert to the family, to remain flexible with respect to the frequency of meetings, to not perceive the family as powerless, and to detect the factors that will allow the family to form a cooperative system with the doctor. The therapist, according to Seeman, teaches the family by deed and by discussion to praise accomplishments in themselves and in the schizophrenic patient, to tolerate feelings without discharging them inappropriately, and to toe the line of familial authority in keeping with the family's own value system.

Following these principles, the *psychoeducational* approach now includes unemotional discussions of how to view the nature of the illness, how to handle the patient during both crisis and remission, how to optimize home management of the illness, how to provide a desirable emotional climate for all family members, how to recognize when the patient is decompensating, how to adopt an attitude of benign indifference at the height of the psychotic thought disorder, how to lower the family's expectations about the patient's future without falling into hopelessness that would lead to self-fulfilling negative prophecies, and how to set firm limits to the behavior of the schizophrenic patient when he or she seriously disrupts family life. Attention is now paid to carefully teaching communication skills so the family can stop addressing each other in an indirect way, through innuendo, through messages that require reading between the lines, or through messages conveyed by the tone of the parent's voice. Family members learn not to talk over each other and to avoid chaos in communication.

The clinician becomes an instructor or traffic controller who educates the family in a polite, orderly way of conversing in order to solve problems. This is easier said than done. Patterns of communication have been with the family for years and, despite great efforts, it takes time to learn new skills and decrease the amount of mutual criticism.

Resistance

At first, some families do not accept a diagnosis of schizophrenia. This creates an initial obstacle the clinician needs to overcome.

Example
Robert, a 19-year-old young man, came alone to the clinic asking for a letter that would enable him to go back to school and take 2 years in one, after being at home for almost 2 years. He expressed great anxiety about performing, especially since he couldn't sleep well at night because he was afraid he was going to damage his own eyes with his fingers. The more I spoke with him, the more I saw the features of a schizophrenic thought disorder. When I subsequently interviewed him with his parents, I saw they were two elderly retired people, previously a construction worker and a nurse, who had taken Robert to faith healers, chiropractors, herb specialists, spiritualists, and a long series of general practitioners, seeking the solution to his "funny ideas" and to his distress. They had allowed him to be practically locked up in his bedroom for a year and a half. When I tried to help them face the diagnosis of schizophrenia and the need for regular medication and perhaps hospitalization, they were shocked and offended. They thought I was condemning their son to a terrible future. The mother, in her days as a nurse, had worked in a chronic psychiatric hospital, and had seen deteriorated schizophrenic patients. "My son is not and will never be like that," she said. The parents accepted a first prescription of phenothiazines for Robert but only irregularly collaborated with the treatment. When I suggested that they join a "Friends of Schizophrenics" organization, they responded: "We do not want to be depressed listening to other people's tragedies. We do not belong to groups like that. We need to hear optimistic

stories, not the stories of crazy people." They withdrew from the clinic where I saw them. Later I was told that they had managed to obtain the letter to allow Robert to take a 2-year course in one, but unfortunately he suffered a breakdown in school and had to be involuntarily hospitalized in extreme agitation.

Family treatment can take place in the home, in the clinic, in the hospital, in the private office of the psychiatrist, or in a social club attended by relatives of schizophrenic patients.

Tasks of the Therapist

Anderson et al. (1980), from whom I quote liberally, summarized the tasks of the therapist as follows: since the schizophrenic individual suffers partly because he or she cannot select relevant stimuli, inhibit irrelevant stimuli, and maintain a functional level of arousal, the clinician's interventions are designed to regulate the stimuli from the environment, including the family interaction. The therapist aims for clarity and acknowledgment in communication, given that communicative behaviors in the family are often vague, amorphous, tangential, or unrelated to the topic at hand. Criticism and emotional overinvolvement have to be decreased to a minimum in order to interrupt the vicious cycle of hyperarousal, disattention, and disease for the patient. The clinician can decrease the family members' anxiety about the patient by increasing their self-confidence and their knowledge about the illness and by enhancing their ability to react constructively to the patient, to simplify the family environment, to diminish chaos, and to promote individual growth. Rules of interaction have to be clear and expectations reasonable; boundaries between generations have to be effective and clear. The family has to learn to be less reactive to provocations and more respectful of their need and the patient's need for distance. The therapist has to take a deliberately simplistic and authoritative stance, trying to elaborate with the family a "road map"; otherwise he or she can be overwhelmed by the at times complicated communication of families of schizophrenic patients (Schaffer et al. 1962). It is useless to give the family sympathy without direction. The clinician has to understand the family's pain, frustration, embarrassment, anger, and guilt; too rapid reassurance may be viewed as insincere and will decrease the clinician's credibility.

During the family sessions, no family member is allowed to speak for another, and no family member is permitted to lose emotional or physical control. The therapist has to stop the sessions or ask one of the members to leave the room if necessary, in order to maintain the order and constructiveness of each family meeting. It has to be stressed to the family that there is no firm evidence that families "cause" schizophrenia; however, we have reason to believe that the family has the power to influence the course of the illness. The relatives of the patient have to strike a balance between realism and hope in terms of their expectations about the schizophrenic family member. If the expectations are too low, the family risks fostering passivity and regression. If the expectations are too high, the family risks promoting anxiety and frustration in everyone. Regression in both the patient and the family are to be expected off and on, whenever there is an increase in pressure due to the vicissitudes of life. The clinician has to aim for one small change at a time and show respect for the limitations and the defenses of the patient and the relatives.

The emancipation of the patient, even though desirable, is particularly upsetting for the family and for the schizophrenic patient and must be handled with great care. The therapist may have to organize maintenance sessions and wait for a prolonged period before any benefits of the intervention are seen. If the first phases of the psychoeducational treatment are successful, there is an option to involve the family in other forms of family therapy, with increased expression of feeling, increased therapeutic pressure, and increased responsibility of family members for the therapy and their participation in it. Grunebaum and Friedman (1988), after commenting on how some therapists fail to be concerned with parents and spouses as people in their own right, highlight five therapeutic tasks in the contact with the family:

1. To ensure that the family has a chance to be heard and to relate their own account of the patient's illness, his or her life, and the life of the family, given that the family's way of experiencing social reality will determine how they work with the clinician, with the hospital, and with each other.
2. To impart information. The clinician should avoid being vague and answer questions as clearly and directly as possible. If the clinician avoids answering questions, he or she alienates and frightens the family. Sometimes the clinician can only give educated guesses. This is better than trying to be safe and vague. The better informed the family is about the illness and its treatment, the more likely they are to follow through on collaborative plans.
3. To help families with the feelings engendered by the patient's illness, the hospitalization, and the treatment efforts. This is aimed again at relieving their uncertainty and fear, their anger directed toward the treatment teams, the self-blame, the projected blame, and the experience of having been blamed by other professionals. Attention must be given to the depression and chronic grief engendered by the loss of hope and the uncertainty of the future of the schizophrenic family member. Elderly parents especially agonize about the future of their psychotic child after they are gone.
4. To identify if the family uses denial, excessive control and intrusiveness, or separateness and distance as coping mechanisms.
5. To assist the family in facing the ethical and existential dilemmas presented by the need to balance their obligations to the ill family member with their own needs.

Example
Mrs. A, a 55-year-old woman diagnosed as paranoid schizophrenic since age 35, was brought to a family evaluation by her

two adult sons, their wives, and her husband. The complaints were the following: The sons were irritated with some annoying habits that their mother had. She kept moving her legs incessantly, sometimes pacing back and forth. She would sleep into the morning, stay awake watching television programs until very late at night, refuse to take her medication, and refuse to visit the psychiatrist. She was unable to speak rationally with anyone in the family. An added element of tragedy in this family was the fact that another son had recently committed suicide and the whole family was unable to talk about it for fear of triggering psychotic symptoms in the mother. Whenever she talked about the dead young man, she would say that she could hear him talk to her and that he was not dead. The patient's husband was a sad, 60-year-old man who had given up the idea of participating in his wife's treatment. He would allow her to talk to herself, sleep as much as she wanted, and stay up as late as she wanted. He would not insist that she take her medication, nor would he bring her to her psychiatric appointments; he spent most of his time attending to his own endeavors, gardening or reading. The adult sons led their own lives with their wives and only sporadically saw the elderly couple; the sons were clearly annoyed about their mother's continuing regression.

The family was slowly educated in clinical matters. They grew to understand that akathisia (motor restlessness the patient finds impossible to stop) and some of their mother's other behavior was a result of the medication she irregularly took. They learned to appreciate that some of their mother's ideas were metaphors to express her yearning for her dead son—a logical response to the isolation in which she found herself, given that her husband had pretty much given up on her. Through educating the family and involving all of them as partial caretakers, the therapist taught them to participate actively in stimulating the patient, preventing her from being alone with her symptoms, and, at times, insisting that she take her medication and attend her psychiatric appointments. The sons had left this task exclusively to their father who, in his hopelessness, had not been active enough in promoting the health of the mother. Not wanting to disturb his sons, the father had resigned himself to live silently with the psychotic behavior of his wife. He certainly avoided hostility and criticism in the home, yet he did not provide human interaction to help the patient out of her psychotic process. The family therapist stressed the patient's strengths: she took good physical care of herself and was able to carry out her household chores. Her habit of getting up very late and staying up to watch television programs until very late was reinterpreted, not as an annoying rebellious act, but as a reasonable alternative since in the mornings she had little reason to get up and encountered almost no human interaction. Television probably provided her with the only stimulation she received, since her husband avoided her. After a few psychoeducational and supportive sessions, the father felt empowered to be more active, less masochistic, and less hopeless about his wife's illness. The sons, while carrying on with their lives, became more active in telephoning frequently, taking turns in being with their mother or taking her out, and making sure she was taking her medication and attending her psychiatric follow-up interviews. The overall functioning of the family became less somber and more hopeful, and the symptoms of the patient were controlled. It has now been 1 year since they were seen, and there has been no relapse of the acute psychosis.

Family Burden

Families perceive the care of their chronically mentally ill relatives as a burden, especially when they do not succeed in communicating well with mental health professionals (Griffin et al. 1988). When the family has to negotiate crisis situations or act as a patient's advocate or a case manager, or try to obtain adequate community resources, continuity of care, and information, and when family members deal with legal problems, they often have difficulty in communicating clearly with mental health professionals and physicians. It is the responsibility of the therapist to reduce that family burden by helping families to improve their communication skills with professionals while, at the same time, improving his or her own skills in communicating with the family. Treatment decisions must include family members and changes in mental health laws should be discussed with them.

Advice to Families

Seeman et al. (1982b, 1984) and Thornton et al. (1985, 1988), in four excellent pamphlets and in their short book *Living and Working With Schizophrenia* (Seeman et al. 1982a), offer many practical suggestions to help families of schizophrenic patients deal with their relatives at home. Among them are what to do when different professionals give the family contradictory advice, how to establish the priority of goals given that self-sufficiency is the main concern in these cases, how to decide what is crucial and requires prodding the patient and what can wait, how to implement initially enjoyable tasks and simple routines to facilitate the recovery of the schizophrenic patient after a breakdown, when to call the police for help, and when to plan a separation requiring the schizophrenic patient to leave the family home for a boarding home or a group home. The book also offers some advice for the clinician when the family asks him or her to keep secret from the schizophrenic patient the concerns they have shared. The authors suggest that attention must be given to the embarrassment and shame families experience when they need to involve other relatives, the police, community agencies, general practitioners, or specialists in times of crisis. For the family, asking for help means admitting that they have been unable to cope alone with the stress of living with a schizophrenic family member.

One last clinical vignette will illustrate some of the problems described above.

Example

The R family sought consultation in our hospital to learn how to manage their 21-year-old son. He was an obese, mildly retarded, schizophrenic young man who had been carefully protected by the parents all his life and had managed to get through primary and high school due to the respect and compassion that his parents commanded in the community. The father was a highly respected teacher and the mother an active benefactor in their ethnic group. The behavior of the son had escalated in increasing aggressiveness and domination of the whole family. During the second family interview, he attempted to establish an argument with me, wanting me to support his wish to enter medical school to become a famous doctor. The absurdity of his argument, laced with intense anxiety, was something that the parents were trying to counteract with reasoning and logical arguments. I felt I needed to demonstrate the attitude of benevolent neglect that theory advocates. I stopped attending to the son, half-turned my back on him (which socially could be considered quite impolite), and addressed the parents: "This is an example of thought disorder. Your son is trying to preserve his self-esteem and that is why he is talking in this way. At moments like this, there is no argument that can defuse his wish to prove that he is worthwhile." I did not know if the young man would react violently to my response. Fortunately, he calmed down. The fact that I stopped paying attention to him seemed to diminish his anxiety and the impetus of his psychotic rambling, and the parents learned *in vivo* how to deal with difficult moments when their psychotic son involved them in his thought disorder. The parents became painfully aware of how psychotic their son was, a fact they had been denying for a long time. They agreed to hospitalize him and began to recognize his limitations.

Other Current Therapies

Beels and McFarlane (1982), in a brief review of approaches to the family when one of the members is schizophrenic, include 1) behavioral training for the family and management advice during home visits (Falloon et al. 1981), centering on the objectives outlined here; and 2) the brief family therapy proposed by Goldstein and Kopeikin (1981), in which the clinician identifies the stressors that disturb the patient and the family, and the habitual mechanisms used to avoid and cope with such stressors. After stress-management training, subsequent assessment is necessary to evaluate whether the learned techniques are now effective. The anticipatory planning Goldstein suggests helps the family think about likely situations in which they will be subjected to stressors and plan beforehand how they will deal with them.

I will end this chapter by mentioning two types of family therapy with schizophrenic patients that I do not advise for the clinician who is working alone. One is the Strategic Family Therapy of Haley (1980) and Madanes (1981), which proposes 1) clarifying hierarchical incongruity in the family, 2) helping parents regain authority over the patient, so the young person can resume the aborted project of "leaving home," and 3) promoting negotiations about household rules and expectations for behavior change. This approach is better applied when working in a team and with hospitalization available in case the interventions precipitate crises that may not be manageable at home. The other type of family therapy that is best practiced with a trained team is the Systemic Family Therapy of Selvini-Palazzoli et al. (1978), which consists of studying the homeostatic self-sacrificing behavior of all participants in the family system and then recommending no change, or stasis, as an empathic response to force members to invent their own escape from the stifling family system. This paradoxical approach, in my opinion, carries considerable risks in inexperienced hands and cannot be implemented by a psychiatrist working alone. The psychoeducational rules proposed in this chapter are more appropriate for the office practice of an individual clinician who attempts to help the family of a schizophrenic patient.

References

Ackerman NW: The Psychodynamics of Family Life. New York, Basic Books, 1958

Ackerman NW: Treating the Troubled Family. New York, Basic Books, 1966

Anderson CM, Hogarty GE, Reiss DJ: Family treatment of adult schizophrenic patients: a psychoeducational approach. Schizophr Bull 6:490–505, 1980

Atwood N, Williams ME: Group support for the families of the mentally ill. Schizophr Bull 4:415–425, 1978

Bateson G, Jackson D, Haley J, et al: Toward a theory of schizophrenia. Behav Sci 1:251–264, 1956

Beels CC, McFarlane WR: Family treatments of schizophrenia: background and state of the art. Hosp Community Psychiatry 33:541–550, 1982

Brown GW, Birley JLT, Wing JH: The influence of family life on the course of schizophrenic disorders: a replication. Br J Psychol 121:241–258, 1972

Dearth N, Labensky BJ, Mott ME, et al: Families Helping Families: Living With Schizophrenia. New York, WW Norton, 1986

Falloon IR II, Boyd JL, McGill GW, et al: Family management training in the community care of schizophrenia, in New Developments in Interventions With Families of Schizophrenics. Edited by Goldstein M. San Francisco, CA, Jossey-Bass, 1981

Goldstein MJ, Kopeikin HS: Short- and long-term effects of combining drug and family therapy, in New Developments in Interventions With Families of Schizophrenics. Edited by Goldstein M. San Francisco, CA, Jossey-Bass, 1981

Gottesman I, Shields J: Schizophrenia: The Epigenetic Puzzle. New York, Cambridge University Press, 1982

Griffin CF, Conn VS, Gray DP: Families' perceptions of burden of care for chronic mentally ill relatives. Hosp Community Psychiatry 39:1296–1300, 1988

Grunebaum H, Friedman H: Building collaborative relationships with families of the mentally ill. Hosp Community Psychiatry 39:1183–1187, 1988

Haley J: Leaving Home: The Therapy of Disturbed Young People. New York, McGraw-Hill, 1980

Langsley DG, Pittman FS, Machotka P, et al: Family crisis therapy: results and implications. Fam Process 7:145–159, 1968

Laqueur HP, LaBart HA, Morony E: Multiple family therapy. Curr Psychiatr Ther 4:150–154, 1964

Lidz T, Cornelison A, Fleck S, et al: The intrafamilial environment of schizophrenic patients, II: marital schism and marital skew. Am J Psychiatry 114:241–248, 1957

Lidz T, Cornelison A, Terry D, et al: Intrafamilial environment of the schizophrenic patient, VI: the transmission of irrationality. Archives of Neurology and Psychiatry 79:305–316, 1958

Madanes C: Strategic Family Therapy. San Francisco, CA, Jossey-Bass, 1981

Schaffer L, Wynne LC, Day J, et al: On the nature and sources of the psychiatrist's experience with the family of the schizophrenic. Psychiatry 25:32–45, 1962

Seeman MV, Littmann SK, Plummer E, et al: Living and Working With Schizophrenia. Toronto, University of Toronto Press, 1982a

Seeman MV, Thornton JF, Plummer E: Schizophrenia: Returning Home. Concord, Ontario, Merrell Pharmaceuticals, 1982b

Seeman MV, Thornton JF, Plummer E: Schizophrenia: Symptoms and Management at Home. Concord, Ontario, Merrell Pharmaceuticals, 1984

Selvini-Palazzoli M, Boscolo L, Cecchin G, et al: Paradox and Counterparadox: A New Model of the Therapy of the Family in Schizophrenic Transaction. New York, Jason Aronson, 1978

Singer MT, Wynne IC: Thought disorder and family relations of schizophrenics, IV: results and implications. Arch Gen Psychiatry 12:201–212, 1965

Thornton JF, Seeman MV, Plummer E, et al: Schizophrenia: The Medications. Concord, Ontario, Merrell Pharmaceuticals, 1985

Thornton JF, Seeman MV, Plummer E, et al: Schizophrenia: Rehabilitation. Concord, Ontario, Merrell Pharmaceuticals, 1988

Vaughn CE, Leff JT: The influence of family and social factors on the course of psychiatric illness. Br J Psychiatry 129: 125–137, 1976

Chapter 6

Group Therapy

PAUL GOLDHAMER, M.D., F.R.C.P.(C)
MOLYN LESZCZ, M.D., F.R.C.P.(C)

Chapter 6

Group Therapy

*L*oneliness and alienation are central problems faced by the individual with schizophrenia. Schizophrenic individuals often long for contact with others but inhibit themselves from initiating it because of fears of rejection and estrangement. At times, human relations are distorted by psychotic ideation. The patient's withdrawal often belies an exquisite sensitivity to interpersonal stimuli. The group setting is an ideal one in that it both illuminates these difficulties and provides an opportunity to address them. Another consideration with respect to the prescription of group therapy is the schizophrenic patient's lifetime challenge of dealing with a chronic mental illness that often requires a treatment that is ongoing and open-ended. This chapter elaborates on the specific role of group psychotherapy in the treatment of schizophrenic patients.

Rationale

The clinician's use of group therapy is influenced by reports of effectiveness of this modality. Although recent reviews (Kanas 1986; Mosher and Keith 1979) document some limitations in research methodology, there appear to be clear areas of positive outcome. Important questions to evaluate include, What kind of group therapy is being utilized? What is the duration of treatment? What is the composition of the group—are patients acutely ill or more chronically ill? The best results occur in the longer-term therapy of chronic schizophrenic patients treated in groups that are interactive. Insight-oriented groups are ineffective and at times can be noxious. The acutely psychotic patient often deteriorates in groups due to the overstimulation and anxiety that arise in such a setting.

Reviewing the literature, Kanas (1986) concluded that in comparison to individual follow-up, group psychotherapy with schizophrenic patients offered the following advantages: 1) There appeared to be a significant reduction in readmission rates; 2) treatment compliance was higher in patients treated with group therapy; 3) there was enhanced social effectiveness and a significant reduction in manifest symptomatology as reflected by rating scales (SES; BPRS); 4) staff morale and job satisfaction were greater, and even in those instances where there were no objective measures of better outcome, both patients and staff preferred group psychotherapy to individual psychotherapy; and 5) group aftercare was more efficient than individual follow-up.

In all instances, the role of group therapy is adjunctive to that of pharmacotherapy. Medication addresses only a segment of disability (Kahn 1984) and as May (1976) suggests, the psychosocial therapies, including group therapy, are complementary to the pharmacotherapies. We believe it is also unproductive to consider individual and group therapy as competing modalities. Rather, the issue in practice is how these modalities can enhance one another, and how to select the optimal methods for each individual patient.

Heterogeneity of the Group Therapies

There is a wide range of experiences labeled group therapy. In fact, a distinction has been made between group therapy and groups that are therapeutic (Mosher and Keith 1980). Criteria for group therapy have been delineated to include: 1) having a group of troubled people gather together for some therapeutic goal; 2) having an expert leader present to assist the group; and 3) exploration of relationships and interactions between group members as a tool for clarification, motivation, or behavior change. In contrast, many groups such as self-help or activity groups may be therapeutic without fulfilling one or more of these criteria. Different names are used to designate this orientation, such as rap groups, coffee and education groups, and group pharmacotherapy (Payn 1965). Payn labeled his approach group pharmacotherapy to distinguish it from group psychotherapy, and he emphasizes that carrying out pharmacotherapy in a group can contribute to patients developing an interest in other people, even though at first there is no interaction between members of the group. Other authors, as will be detailed in the following sections, do focus on and interpret group interactions and employ traditional, albeit modified group therapy techniques.

Even within an apparently homogeneous group designation, there are heterogeneous needs, capacities, and personalities of patients to consider. The range of group treatments may include a fairly stable, interactive, verbal group of 6–10 patients who meet long term; a group that focuses mostly on activities and outings with a de-emphasis on verbal interaction, and in which interpersonal connection is a byproduct of the structure; and a form of drop-in or rap group, open to whomever, whenever, within the purview of a particular institution (Tozman et al. 1981). Groups may meet within offices of private practitioners or in clinic settings, in which case the institutional transference is accentuated as a way to further maintain group cohesiveness. The office practitioner is more likely to have a more stable population treated with more verbal means, but even in this setting for these patients, authors recommend more direct gratification of dependency needs through the provision of snacks and social interaction before and after group sessions.

O'Brien (1975) suggests larger groups (8 to 12) for more withdrawn patients and smaller groups (6 to 8) for more expressive patients who can tolerate more closeness. He recommends limiting the number of very paranoid individuals in the group to no more than 1 or 2 because they are disruptive to the group and interfere with the development of group cohesiveness. A common situation in clinic settings is to have a group with a roster of 20 to 40 patients, with the expectation that only 6 to 12 will appear at weekly meetings. A core group that carries the group cohesiveness may emerge and the other patients come when they are in crisis or in need of support, or at prescribed minimum frequency to monitor medication. It is useful for the therapist to maintain an appropriate therapeutic perspective and have realistic goals that expect neither too little nor too much, yet recognize the diversity of function in the schizophrenic population.

If the patients selected for the group are more chronic, less interactive, and less articulate about themselves, the goals of the group will be more modest. These goals would include: 1) having patients attend the group with peers regularly, to minimize feelings of isolation and enhance a sense of belonging; 2) offering patients an opportunity to develop and practice social skills at a behavioral level; and 3) providing group reinforcement for the necessary health-promoting behaviors such as attending the group, taking medication, and avoiding harmful situations such as street drugs. Meetings need to be highly structured. This kind of group normally would meet weekly for 60 minutes with snacks and social interaction afforded both before and after the meeting.

For patients who have greater interpersonal and introspective capacities, the group's goals may be more extensive and may include: 1) enhancing social interaction and opportunity for engagement; 2) helping patients give and receive help from others, generating the benefits of raising self-esteem through altruism; 3) learning to detect early emergence of psychotic symptoms and reacting by making appropriate changes in obtaining necessary treatment (this enhances reality testing and therapeutic compliance); 4) developing strategies to master psychotic experiences (Seeman 1988); and 5) recognizing and changing maladaptive behaviors, which may lead to improved social relationships. The group goals may be more modest early in the group's life but may become more ambitious over time as members grow more secure and comfortable within the group. A group such as this typically meets once weekly in the practitioner's office for 60–90 minutes and has a more stable composition of regular attenders. It is open-ended and long-term and may attend more to the group process and not be focused entirely on the content as in the former instance. The differentiation in goals and objectives is, however, relative rather than absolute. In both instances, emphasis is on enhancing social interaction and increasing interpersonal engagement, albeit directly with the healthier patients or indirectly with the less well patients.

Selection and Preparation of Patients

The techniques used in a group depend on the patients selected for the group and the goals that are set. Kanas et al. (1988) strongly advocate homogeneous groups for schizophrenic patients to protect the patients from feelings of further estrangement from peers or rejection following the expression of bizarre or psychotic symptomatology. Their feeling is that homogeneous groups facilitate more openness regarding disclosure of the psychotic process. Homogeneous groups also facilitate the discussion of issues related to medications, side effects, and compliance. However, it is wise not to be bound by diagnosis alone but rather to attend to level of ego function, as, for example, O'Brien (1975) does in his differentiation between the withdrawn schizophrenic patient and the more active schizophrenic patient. On occasion a schizophrenic patient in remission may be treated in a group of nonschizophrenic individuals. This should be done only with careful consideration to the vulnerability of such a patient to overstimulation. Strassberg et al. (1975) document that self-disclosure can be stimulated among schizophrenic patients by virtue of prompting and reinforcement but that this often leads to patient deterioration. More may be stimulated than can in fact be integrated by the patient. Techniques that would be useful for nonpsychotic patients may be noxious at times for the psychotic patient.

Factors to consider in patient assessment, selection, and the determination of what type of group is suitable include: 1) Do all the members have a diagnosis of schizophrenia? 2) Are they aware of the diagnosis? 3) Are they interested in learning more about their illness? 4) Are they able and willing to share their experiences of illness and the impact of illness on their lives with others in the group? 5) Are they willing to come to weekly or only to monthly meetings? 6) What are their hopes for the group—education, growth, friendship, or support? 7) What capacity and interest have they shown in developing and maintaining relationships with family, friends, therapists in the past? 8) If their capacity for verbal interaction is very limited, what forms of activity might they enjoy?

In all instances, it is useful to prepare patients before entry into the group. Although the effectiveness of pregroup training has not yet been researched with the schizophrenic population, it has been proven effective with every patient population studied to date. Proper pretherapy training enhances group tenure and adherence to group task, diminishes pathological anxiety, raises enthusiasm for the group, and in general enhances the therapeutic alliance (Yalom 1985). Preparation includes providing the patient with a detailed overview of how the group operates, its rationale, the group norms, what the patient can expect, and what will be required of him or her. It is useful to stress the inherent benefits of the group therapy and not to highlight its economic considerations. No one wants a perceived cut-rate therapy.

Despite appropriate preparation, there can be resistance both to entry to the group and, once in the group, to maintaining a stable ongoing commitment to a cohesive group. Often a therapist will consider a patient very suitable for a group but the patient will be reluctant to attend.

Example
Sarah is a 42-year-old single woman with a diagnosis of schizophrenia. She has persistently refused to take medication and experiences religious delusions—typically that God talks to her,

offering her advice and support by indirect messages. She maintains these delusions in an encapsulated form, not telling anyone but her individual therapist. She is able to hold a job in a bookstore but wishes she could have a more active social life. In response to this wish for more social engagement, her individual therapist suggested adding group therapy to her treatment. She refused, stating that she feared someone else in the group might disclose experiences with God similar to hers, and she would feel less special if this were so.

In addition to these psychotic resistances, there are nonpsychotic resistances to engagement in the group. For some patients, the idea of participation in a group will remain too threatening to allow group participation.

Example
Tom was a 36-year-old divorced man with a 10-year history of schizophrenia. For the first 7 years of his illness, he had many hospitalizations as well as arrests for aggressive public behavior in response to command hallucinations. Over the past 3 years he has been seen individually in supportive psychotherapy. During this time he has been stable with no need for hospitalization, but has continued to experience occasional psychotic symptoms and to lead a very isolated life. In individual meetings, Tom is articulate about his personal experiences, but when his therapist suggested that he participate in a group led by this therapist, as an adjunct to the individual meetings, Tom resisted strongly. He stated that he was afraid of getting involved with others and being disappointed—"It would be like entering a marriage knowing it would end in 2 years, so why do it?" This fixed time length was clearly his own creation, no doubt reflecting his prior experience of marriage, which ended abruptly after 2 years when his wife left him for another man. In addition to this fear of ultimate abandonment, he expressed a fear of displaying an ugly side of himself to others and to his therapist. In individual sessions he expresses a range of feelings but is invariably soft-spoken and polite. In a group setting, he believed he would become "hard, aggressive, and sarcastic."

With some patients, specifically identifying the cause of the resistance may allow reframing it into the very reason the group treatment is indicated. This may lead to a gradual fading of the resistance and a willingness to risk the new experience of a group.

Practical Considerations in the Conduct of the Group

At the outset of the group, therapists should decide on ground rules and clearly convey these to the members. This includes consideration of the frequency and length of sessions, goals, expectations for members and therapists concerning attendance and participation, and rules concerning extragroup contact. In a group aiming to promote self-understanding and improved interpersonal functioning, members are expected to attend all sessions. This would typify a group of schizophrenic patients in a private practice group. In groups of more chronic patients, often clinic based, members may choose when to attend.

If possible, it is useful to have a cotherapy team, representing therapists from different disciplines in addition to psychiatry, notably nursing, occupational therapy, or social work. This cotherapy model provides the members with two perspectives on issues and two role models with whom to identify, especially in cases of mixed-sex cotherapy teams. In addition, cotherapy provides the therapists with support for each other, often necessary at times of group resistance or demoralization. It ensures that despite therapists' vacations or absences, at least one therapist will be present at each scheduled meeting, mitigating against the likelihood of cancellation of groups with the resultant deleterious effect on group cohesion and affiliation.

In most standard psychodynamic psychotherapy groups, extragroup contact is strongly discouraged due to the risks of subgrouping, secret alliances, and the resultant anticohesive effect on the group (Yalom 1985). With the schizophrenic patient, extragroup contact can be quite beneficial. This contact can address directly the real need for relationships and for some patients may be the only social interaction they have. In these instances, emphasis should be placed not upon prohibiting extragroup contact but rather prohibiting any secrecy about the extragroup contact. Similarly, it is worthwhile to set as a norm the idea that all members of the group can participate in the extragroup contact, to avoid subgroups or cliques. For instance, after each group, the members of the group may regularly go out for coffee and enjoy a continuation of their discussion in a more informal manner. However, group therapists encourage the discussion of relevant issues that arise outside the group within the group.

Example

Two patients complained to the group therapist in their individual sessions about the behavior of a third member of the group, Joan, at the restaurant. She talked in a loud voice about her psychotic experiences and frequent hospitalizations, embarrassing the others in public. They were encouraged to discuss this issue in the next group meeting, which they did. This led to a useful session dealing with the issues of private and public behavior, with whom one can share personal feelings and experiences, and the importance of protecting the group's confidentiality.

Group and individual therapy may be provided concurrently, although many patients will benefit from group therapy alone. When applied concurrently, patients may be seen by the same group and individual therapist (combined therapy) or by a different group and individual therapist (conjoint therapy). Iatrogenic difficulties may arise if the group leader sees some of the members of the group individually and not others, as the patients who do not have individual sessions may feel excluded or feel jealous and inferior. Hence in combined group and individual therapy the group should be homogeneous for this factor.

With vulnerable patients it may be useful at times to be able to process the experience of the group outside of the group in an individual session, if it is too overwhelming to do so within the group. It is imperative in this instance, however, that the material discussed outside of the group ultimately be brought back to its proper forum. In conjoint treatment, this happens more readily when the individual and group therapist approach the patient similarly, are noncompetitive between themselves, and have respect for the contributions of both treatments. The absence of these factors stands as a relative contraindication to concurrent treatment.

Example
Joan suggested in a group meeting that members could develop feelings of closeness to one another by practicing social exercises, including hugging. Another member, Tony, groaned, and the others laughed at his groan. Joan did not comment on this behavior but told her individual therapist that she felt hurt. She was encouraged to speak about this in the next meeting rather than remain hurtfully silent, which she would do if left to herself. Later, she was pleased at her ability to be assertive and valued Tony's explanation that he did not mean to insult her or offend her, but rather he was enjoying playing the clown as he typically does.

With more withdrawn and less verbal patients, groups will need to be structured to provide a nonthreatening, social experience. Providing refreshments such as coffee and juice and cookies promotes a more relaxed informal atmosphere. In one clinic group, the members decided to label their group the "friendship group" and extended the menu to sandwiches, pizza, and ice cream. In the office setting, the desired atmosphere is more formal as the goals usually extend beyond friendship to interpersonal learning, and in these instances food preparation and consumption would be distracting. One compromise is for the members of the group to work in a formal manner in the office and then go out for coffee together (without the therapist) for lighter and more social conversation. Additionally, it is desirable to select patients who are likely to relapse less frequently and are able to benefit from an approach that promotes more interpersonal engagement and some self-understanding. A smaller group size of 5 to 7 members is suitable for the office practitioner who is more likely to work without a cotherapist. With fewer members it becomes particularly important to emphasize regular attendance, because an absent or relapsing member can be disruptive to the group functioning. The smaller, more stable group often leads to increased cohesion with strong loyalties developing among members and to the group.

It is essential that the therapist not devalue nondepth approaches in favor of treatments aimed at changing core personality or disease processes. At the same time, expecting too little or tolerating too much regression is a therapeutic error. The therapist must continually reassess his or her own therapeutic perspective to ensure that he or she is responding to the patient accurately in terms of level and potential. With more withdrawn patients, the therapist needs to select topics for discussion, allow members to direct their responses to the familiar therapist, draw out nonparticipating members with a go-round of opinions and feelings, all the while avoiding threatening issues such as competition and aggression between members. Fenn and Dinaburg (1981), for example, cite success using a didactic model in which the group initially forms around issues of education and discussion regarding symptoms of the illness and medication. They take a self-help approach to illness and expect very little at first by way of interpersonal engagement, emphasizing rather the patient's relationship with the therapist in dealing with a serious illness together. These groups will rarely operate in the realm of the here-and-now and will focus more on content than on process.

Higher functioning groups of patients can be encouraged to interact more with one another by the therapist's explicit reinforcement of such interaction and his or her stimulation of direct communication. Interaction can also be fostered by techniques such as role playing, in which two or three members enact familiar situations such as dealing with employers and social agencies. Other techniques aimed at generating intimacy too quickly should be avoided as these are almost always intimidating and threatening to the schizophrenic patient. These groups may focus on the here-and-now in terms of the interpersonal interactions between and among members of the group. The emphasis on process may predominate over that on content, and the need for the therapist to structure the group may diminish. These are guidelines, and the therapist needs to be attuned to the level of anxiety in the group, at times deepening the work, and at other times in true ego-supportive fashion diluting, deintensifying, or de-emphasizing highly charged areas of group discussion.

In all groups of schizophrenic patients, the therapist is quite active and directive in his or her efforts at maximizing participation by all members, limiting monopolization by grandiose members, and reinforcing and shaping desirable patient-to-patient behavior. The requirements on the therapist in this kind of group are much greater than in a group of healthier, more intact individuals, and the group therapist is often an important anchor in the development of group cohesiveness. He or she must recognize and accept this burden rather than wait for the group to activate itself. Silence is rarely therapeutic in such groups, and shifting all the responsibility for initiation and engagement onto the group members may often lead to group resistance, patient disengagement, and therapeutic failure.

The Process of Group Therapy

A variety of important therapeutic mechanisms and issues are generated within the group. Medication may be a primary and ongoing focus in the population of patients who are more ill or it may be an initial and transient focus in groups of higher functioning schizophrenic patients. Much feeling regarding medication may emerge in both instances, related not only to discussion of side effects but also to discussion of dosages and, in particular, dose reductions. There may be feelings of competitiveness or envy that if left unchecked could lead to abrupt cessation of medication, which is a risk for the schizophrenic patient in any instance. Working through such issues enhances treatment compliance and also avoids the abrupt unilateral cessation of medication.

The group therapy objectives of fostering interpersonal interaction, supporting reality testing, and mastering psychotic experiences are often interwoven. This is especially so when the presence of psychotic perceptions and experiences distorts human relatedness.

Example

In a stable ongoing group, Debbie, a 32-year-old female chronic schizophrenic, burst out in anger at one of the group's coleaders for his previous absence and in general his perceived lack of warmth and accessibility. After a brief but furious discharge, she appeared preoccupied. She described to the group auditory hallucinations that were frightening to her. Voices were saying that they were going to kill her, and she began to hallucinate actively in the group. A copatient, Donald, a schizophrenic man who had been stable for an extended period of time, responded by saying that the hallucinations were a reaction to her intense anger, a phenomenon that he experienced many times before. He reminded her that there was nothing wrong in speaking about what she felt, and that it would not lead to anyone getting destroyed or hurt. This kind of empathic support from someone "who has been there" is one of the very powerful ways of detoxifying a frightening psychotic experience. Other group members also encouraged her forthrightness, and the cotherapist was able, quite appropriately, to say that rather than feeling angry, he was relieved that she drew attention to the fact that she was feeling neglected by him. He reframed it to be a statement about her wish for more reliable contact and access with him and within the group—an objective both the group leaders and group patients endorsed fully.

In this instance, the group's accurately empathic support and confrontation of the psychotic regression and distortion in reality served to contain effectively the psychotic experience, leading to rapid resolution and symptom abatement.

Example

In another group, a chronically psychotic man named Sam entered the group with much agitation. He announced that he was going to be forced to move to a hostel because of changes in his group home. He was upset and frightened. However, instead of speaking about that, he stated that if he indeed were forced to go to this hostel, he would bring onto the hospital the fury of Satan, and hellfire and brimstone would engulf the clinic. He went on at some length and initially the group was reeling, not knowing how to respond to him. The therapist suggested that Sam check out with the group what people were feeling toward him at this moment. What followed was their statement of concern for him but that they had nothing to say to him in terms of his threats of destruction. With some questioning by the therapist, they began to feed back to Sam that talking about fire, hell, and brimstone precluded anyone taking him seriously, while in fact he had a serious complaint. They were able then to get him to focus on his particular and realistic concerns. Sam spoke about the lack of security and safety in the hostel. Leaving the group home would make him vulnerable to assault and to theft. The group immediately responded, saying that these were legitimate concerns that anyone could understand, and if he could voice them directly in this fashion his credibility would be significantly enhanced. For the rest of the group, Sam worked on how he would approach his social worker to make these points clear in such a way that he would be understood as "a man asking for human, realistic supplies" rather than someone who was completely out of touch with reality.

The group provides patients with an opportunity to give of themselves to others by virtue of offering support, advice, and understanding. This often results in mutual feelings of appreciation and a feeling of helpfulness and competence on the part of the support giver. Schizophrenic patients often feel that their status as "mental patients" devalues them and invalidates their ability to be effective and useful to others. The bipolarity of altruism and low self-worth oscillate in the group, providing useful material for discussion. Raising one's self-esteem through the act of helping another is a highly valued therapeutic factor (Kanas et al. 1988) and is also a central factor in the action of mastery over a chronic illness, in a fashion similar to that reported in self-help groups.

Example
Gloria talked to the group about her discouragement in her vocational rehabilitation program. Others related similar experiences in which they felt demoralized and demeaned in such programs. They said these programs often were superficial and were not specifically suited to their needs. Nonetheless, the group encouraged Gloria to continue with her work and suggested ways she could approach her supervisor to make the program more gratifying. A comember, Kent, was particularly supportive yet added later, "What good are these suggestions? We're all losers." Gloria chided him for his pessimistic view but thanked him for his earlier useful comments.

Through the process of watching others in the group and seeing examples of their own issues dealt with publicly by other members of the group, a broad range of learning opportunities are accessed. Patients can learn from other group members and not just from the leader, thereby minimizing regressive dependencies on the therapist and diluting the intensity of negative transferences. Relationships between members in the group are often strengthened by mutual discussion of the psychotic illness that they each suffer. Patients learn that they are not alone or unique with their experiences. In addition to learning more about the illness at a cognitive level, it can also be understood in a nonblaming way.

Participating in the group as equal members also serves to enhance feelings of universality and essential alikeness with one another. Accordingly, one can give and receive negative feedback without devastating effects. The presence of supportive peers who will be able to speak in the group to both sides of any conflict anchors the individual patients and promotes greater self-expression. Expressing feelings is another therapeutic factor valued very highly by schizophrenic patients in groups (Kanas et al. 1988). The expression of feelings is best assessed subjectively rather than objectively. A relatively small disclosure, objectively, may be of great significance to the individual. Observations made by patients and feedback from therapists or patients may lead to behavioral change and a broadening of a member's behavioral repertoire. The therapist needs to monitor the way in which feedback is given and received to ensure that no patient is scapegoated or attacked. It may be helpful to emphasize the invitation for behavior that is desired rather than emphasize the rejection of behavior.

Patients' self-acceptance and tolerance of others often increase as patients can see faults in others that are familiar to them and yet enjoy one another's company. Much of what is criticized in others is often a projection of painful and disavowed parts of the self. This may occur within the context of one member of the group rejecting the entire group, or members of the group colluding unconsciously to scapegoat an individual.

Example
After her first three group sessions, Gloria informed the group therapist in an individual session that she wanted to leave the group. She provided a devastatingly accurate and perceptive critique of each member and wondered why she should associate with such people. She was encouraged to stay in the group and to try and understand and relate to each of the individuals more fully before she discarded them. With this encouragement she persisted. She later realized that she felt contemptuous of some members because of her fear of being or becoming like them. For example, Joan was a woman of approximately the same age who had had numerous breakdowns and now accepted a low-key life-style. Gloria was afraid that she would be obliged to give up her drive and ambition in order to accommodate her illness, and this would turn her into a passive, chronic patient as she perceived Joan to be. As she became less frantic in pursuing social and vocational achievements, she became more accepting of herself. She was able to appreciate Joan's virtues, such as her calmness and empathic responses to other members. Several months later Gloria was so enthusiastic about the group that she invited the members to her home for a Christmas party.

A useful lesson for patients to learn is that mental illness is only one facet of a person's existence and need not define that person. When successfully implanted, this attitude leads to greater acceptance of the illness and acceptance of the need for treatment. This reduces feelings of shame and stigmatization associated with being mentally ill and also mitigates against unilateral drug cessation.

Example

Kent repeatedly commented in one way or another in his early sessions in the group, "Why should I belong to any group that wants me as a member?" When he was cynical, he was confronted by others and reassured that he had much to offer. These experiences led him to engage far more in the group therapy than he had in the previous 3 years of individual sessions. When another member was becoming ill, he at first responded in a typically cynical manner, "Why is it such a big deal? You've had so many breakdowns before, you must be used to it." However, in subsequent sessions, he acknowledged that he had been defensively unconcerned because he was feeling so threatened and apprehensive by someone else's potential illness. He was able to discuss more freely his own fear of psychosis as well as his own feelings of loneliness and alienation. At the same time he was wanting to explore for the first time in years how he could make changes in his own life and pursue social and educational goals. After many months, he became quite protective of the group and one of its strongest defenders. At the same time he was becoming more confident and insightful about himself in his individual sessions and more active in his social life.

Group therapy provides a unique arena for dealing with separations and loss of relationships. In the group, members come and go, and it is possible for the remaining members of the group to feel sad, disappointed, and angry without feeling entirely abandoned. The experience of separation can be more constructively dealt with, as the group encourages grieving of a lost relationship in the presence of relationships that do indeed persist. In other situations, losses either are denied or completely overwhelm the process of treatment.

117

Additionally, the group provides an opportunity for mastering psychotic symptomatology (Seeman 1988). Patients are given the benefit of others' experiences in coping and can learn that their symptoms are often reactions to stress or the interplay of the person and his or her environment. The group can catalyze patients to master their symptomatology and accept responsibility for dealing with it rather than externalize the responsibility. This is best achieved when the group identifies and works through those interpersonal or psychosocial factors that contribute to the exacerbation of symptoms—for instance, auditory hallucinations following an expression of anger.

The patient may be able to anticipate stressful situations and react prophylactically or at least minimize deleterious consequences by self-regulation of medication. When it is manifest in the group, effective coping can be reinforced. The stressors facing each individual may be different and, accordingly, coping strategies may be different. Patients can be helped to identify specific strategies such as contacting friends or family, or, conversely, destimulating and pacing themselves.

Group cohesion has been referred to in many of the preceding sections. Its importance, however, warrants further specific notation. Treatment is a slow and long process. Group cohesiveness will develop very slowly and cannot be pushed too quickly. Cohesion-breeding remarks may have paradoxical effects because closeness and engagement may engender anxiety and fears of rejection, abandonment, destructiveness, or dissolution of ego boundaries. The therapist is best advised to move slowly. In a sense, the therapist may need to be more committed to the group at first than its members are. It is often up to the therapist alone to ensure "the presence" of the group by his or her consistency, reliability, and predictability, even, or especially, when it appears to matter very little to the designated members of the group.

Sporadic attendance is to be expected at first. The therapist can make it more appealing for patients to come by providing a social or snack component, what Seeman (1981) describes as "immediate and tangible rewards." Other logistical considerations that enhance attendance include choosing a time that fits most schizophrenic patients' schedules. For instance, a midday meeting close to lunchtime may be the ideal time as opposed to the more typical late afternoon/early evening time of traditional group therapy. This time is less likely to interfere with patients sleeping late or having difficulty getting mobilized in the morning. At the same time, it provides a useful focus for their day.

Despite the best-laid plans of the therapist, some groups take what seems an interminable length of time to come alive (Cohn 1988). Such resistance appears to be related to a need to maintain sameness. New experiences are strongly resisted. Resistance can take the shape of absences, lateness, nonparticipation, contact only with the group leader, or the production of psychotic communications intended to estrange a speaker from the rest of the group. Resistances often relate to the anxiety that the group is expected to operate at too high a level. Resistances emerge in response to any threat to the self of the individuals of the group, or to the boundaries and integrity of the group as a whole. This may be related to any intense affect, competition, or anger. Psychotic behavior and expressions in chronic groups reflect at times not just the phenomenology of the illness but a characteristic way of dealing with anxiety and the reaction to psychological stress. These threats can be addressed by the therapist's support of individual members, confrontation of distortions, and expressing the value he or she sees in the group through his or her behavior and words.

Termination

For many patients, treatment is ongoing and open-ended. Although Kanas et al. (1988) have reported on successful brief group therapy with schizophrenic patients, in general it is not in the therapeutic interest of the patient to set a termination date upon entry into the group. In our clinical experience, groups continue to function in an ego-supportive fashion indefinitely with new members periodically joining and old members leaving. Members who choose to leave make their own decisions about this but are urged to discuss it in advance with the group. For many patients, their involvement with the group may span many years, being centrally involved at certain periods of time and then peripherally involved for another length of time, and then completely absent for another stretch of time.

Conclusion

Groups for patients with schizophrenia encompass a variety of experiences. In some groups, a shared activity such as meal preparation or an outing is the focus. In other groups, patients come to clinics to receive prescriptions and receive advice from their doctor in the presence of other members of the group. More formal group therapy involves a systematic attempt to promote interactions between members and to provide an opportunity to learn from these interactions. In all group activities, the objective is to minimize the schizophrenic patient's inherent feelings of aloneness and estrangement. If successful, the patient engages in more gratifying human experiences and at the same time can gain a sense of mastery over his or her chronic mental disorder.

References

Cohn BR: Keeping the group alive: dealing with resistance in a long-term group of psychotic patients. Int J Group Psychother 38:319–335, 1988

Fenn HH, Dinaburg D: Didactic group psychotherapy with chronic schizophrenics. Int J Group Psychother 31:443–452, 1981

Kahn EM: Group treatment interventions for schizophrenics. Int J Group Psychother 34:149–153, 1984

Kanas N: Group therapy with schizophrenics: a review of controlled studies. Int J Group Psychother 36:339–351, 1986

Kanas N, Stuart P, Haney K: Content and outcome in a short-term therapy group for schizophrenic outpatients. Hosp Community Psychiatry 39:437–439, 1988

May PRA: Rational treatment for an irrational disorder: what does the schizophrenic patient need? Am J Psychiatry 133:1008–1012, 1976

Mosher LR, Keith SJ: Research on the psychosocial treatment of schizophrenia: a summary report. Am J Psychiatry 136:623–631, 1979

Mosher LR, Keith SJ: Psychosocial treatment: individual, group, family and community support approaches. Schizophr Bull 6:10–41, 1980

O'Brien CP: Group therapy for schizophrenia: a practical approach. Schizophr Bull 13:119–129, 1975

Payn SB: Group methods in the pharmacotherapy of chronic psychotic patients. Psychiatr Q 39:258–263, 1965

Seeman MV: Outpatient groups for schizophrenia—ensuring aftercare. Can J Psychiatry 26:32–37, 1981

Seeman MV: Toward mastery of psychotic symptoms: a group phenomenon. Can J Psychiatry 33:702–704, 1988

Strassberg DS, Roback HB, Anchor KJ, et al: Self-disclosure in group therapy with schizophrenics. Arch Gen Psychiatry 32:1259–1261, 1975

Tozman S, Hanks T, Minkowitz HB: The rap group: a milieu treatment model for the chronically ill in an outpatient setting. Int J Group Psychother 31:233–245, 1981

Yalom ID: The Theory and Practice of Group Psychotherapy. New York, Basic Books, 1985

Chapter 7

Antipsychotic Pharmacotherapy

MARY V. SEEMAN, M.D., F.R.C.P.(C)

Chapter 7

Antipsychotic Pharmacotherapy

Most patients suffering from schizophrenia find it necessary to take antipsychotic medication more or less regularly (Davis 1975). There are individuals whose symptoms respond so thoroughly to neuroleptic drugs that they feel completely well while on them. Unfortunately such individuals are in the minority. For most, neuroleptics are a mixed blessing, helping some symptoms while aggravating or causing others. One of the physician's important tasks in the treatment of schizophrenic illness is to be familiar with the medications he or she prescribes. It is also important to be familiar with the patient and with the patient's environmental stressors. It is only by the in-depth knowledge of all three (the patient, the drugs, and the patient's life) that optimal medication adjustment can be achieved. Ideally, this maximizes the person's potential for recovery and minimizes the associated problems. The task is not an easy one. It is as much an art as a science and it necessitates the full cooperation of the patient and the patient's family. In other words, optimal medication adjustment requires a solid patient-doctor relationship of trust and mutual sharing before it can succeed (Goldhamer 1983).

The initial task is to overcome the patient's resistance to drugs (Van Putten 1974). Many individuals hold a strong antidrug attitude, equating all medications with substance abuse (Amarasingham 1980). Alternately, they view drugs as the taking in of foreign substances, with a potential for tolerance, addiction, and long-term harmful effects (Diamond

1985). If their resistance is sufficiently strong, they will require treatment without drugs because token acquiescence usually results in haphazard compliance with the regimen and a lack of openness about drug effects, or lack of them. This often is the explanation for lack of response to a drug. It is best to explore the resistance, understand it, empathize with it, and prolong and maintain the discussion about the pros and cons of drug treatment. Reading material sometimes helps. Explanation of the way drugs work is helpful. Frank discussion of side effects and long-term effects is mandatory. Individuals who do not like taking pills of any sort are best offered a short course, perhaps 3–4 months with a definite date as to when dose tapering and a stop to drugs will ensue. This is much better tolerated than an indefinite attitude of "we'll wait and see."

Example
James, a young artist, had suffered an acute psychotic illness and had been prescribed relatively low doses of antipsychotics that, nevertheless, caused him many unpleasant side effects. He had been a substance abuser in his teens and was now very strongly against pills of all sorts. Though still delusional, he complained bitterly about the continued use of drugs and took them very reluctantly. After much discussion with him, we held a family meeting. His mother, who suffered from rheumatoid arthritis, tried to make the analogy to her own condition and to her own requirement for anti-inflammatory drugs. The analogy was poignantly made but did not budge James from his resolve to stop his drugs. We subsequently worked out a slow drug reduction program with a definite date at which the drugs would stop and we kept to it firmly even though, from my point of view, the medications would have had better effect if taken over a longer period.

The follow-up on James is mixed. He was able to manage drug free for several months, his relationship with me solidified, and he trusted me. He did, however, become more delusional and himself asked to be put back on drugs. Though side effects are presumably as difficult to tolerate now as before, he no longer complains about them. The decision being his seems to have made the difference.

Resistance to drugs is sometimes, perhaps frequently, a form of illness denial (Van Putten 1974). Essentially everyone, when ill, harbors a thought that it is all a mistake, a misdiagnosis, an ailment that will miraculously disappear in the morning. The person with schizophrenia is very prone to this form of magical thinking and is not easily persuaded that his or her set of symptoms is an indication of something seriously wrong. It is easier to think of it as a passing problem, a reaction to someone else's misdeeds. If that is the main issue, it is better to concentrate on one symptom, insomnia for instance, and prescribe medication for that—an acknowledged problem—than to try unsuccessfully to persuade someone that they have an illness that they insist is not there (Tupin 1985).

Example

Barry is a young man who for several years has been preoccupied with the conviction that all the clothing manufacturers in North America have gotten together to prevent him from working. He feels this is connected to the results of a basketball game that is to be played at some time in the future and that will, eventually, vindicate him. In line with this belief, Barry has engaged in difficult-to-understand behavior, often disruptive and even assaultive. He tends to be loud spoken, irritable, and easily moved to anger. His family is afraid of him and wants him to take more and more neuroleptics because these drugs control his behavior and make him more tractable. His mother tends to emphasize the connection between the taking of the drugs and his behavior. This makes him even angrier because he views his behavior as totally appropriate to what he understands is going on around him. He sees nothing out of the way about his actions. He sees nothing wrong with his logic or conclusions. He feels the clothing manufacturers are in league against him, and he cannot see why he should take drugs. His own solution would be to sue the wrongdoers. His constant preoccupations do not allow him to sleep, and he readily accepted medication when it was presented as something that would help him get some sleep, which it did.

Other symptoms for which patients will usually accept medication are headaches, performance anxiety, fears that they acknowledge to be unfounded, and sometimes hallucinations, depending on their understanding of how the hallucinations are produced. As a rule, patients will not accept medication for a symptom they feel is someone else's doing, although sometimes the idea that they are debilitated and easy prey to the wickedness of others may allow them to take something to protect them or make them less vulnerable. Depending on the patient's understanding of the nature of his or her symptoms, I have made the analogy to a sunscreen. The sun, though natural, has harmful effects on the skin with undue exposure. The same can be said of everyday stress. Some skins are more sensitive to the sun's effects than others, just as some individuals are more sensitive to the natural effects of stress than others. Some need more sunscreen than others, depending not only on their type of skin but on previous exposure and adaptation and also on the duration and intensity of exposure. The same variables hold for stress and neuroleptics. When patients acknowledge problems in the past but are unaware of any in the present and cannot see why their neuroleptics should continue, I have made the analogy to brushing and flossing teeth. The toothpaste and floss do not cure cavities and gum disease but, if regularly applied, prevent them from occurring. The same can be said of maintenance neuroleptics.

Many patients refuse neuroleptics because of very legitimate concern with side effects (Van Putten 1974), either those previously experienced or those heard about from others or read about. It is the physician's responsibility to confirm the possibility of such side effects and to instruct the patient on how they might be overcome or prevented. For instance, patients frequently do not realize that most side effects are dose dependent and that problems can be averted by using a low dose regimen or, when indicated, starting with very low doses and increasing the dose by very small increments over time. The rate of change of dose is often responsible for the presence or absence of unwanted effects; if the rate of change is slow, the body adapts (Seeman 1981).

Example
Barry, mentioned earlier, adamantly refused medication except for sleep. In part this was because he did not believe he was ill. In part, it was because he had suffered disfiguring and embarrassing side effects in the past (akathisia, mouth twisting, obesity, bad skin). He accepted something for sleep, found it helped him sleep but also found that it made him feel generally better without producing unwanted side effects. He asked for more. Although we were far from an antipsychotic dose, I chose to increase his dose very, very slowly. This strategy was not welcomed by his family who saw him as grossly psychotic, irritable, and unpleasant to live with. On the other hand, Barry himself felt subjectively better and continued to ask for more medication until, over time, an antipsychotic dose level was finally reached but so gradually that no intolerable side effects emerged.

It has been everybody's experience that medication will be accepted from one nurse and not from another, one doctor but not another, one family member but not another. This speaks to the personal relationship between patient and caregiver and the meaning of medication in the context of that relationship (Adelman 1985). Most often, patients will refuse medications if they are perceived as a power play, an effort by the other party to enforce his or her point of view and to control the patient's freedom. When resistance is traced to interpersonal difficulties, the issue of medication is best left aside until power relationships, motives, and mutual goals are explored and clarified.

Example
Paul refused medication from the ward doctor but took it willingly from the resident who allowed himself to be called by his first name. The issue with the ward doctor was that he insisted on being addressed as "doctor," which, to the patient, meant a stance of authoritativeness and bullying.

Another powerful reason why patients refuse drugs is because they have been to psychiatric hospitals and have known others who have taken these drugs. They view these others as sick, "crazy," and suffering from something very different and much more severe than what they experience themselves. They do not wish to identify with these others by taking the same type of medication. This negative identification can happen even among individuals who have never been to the hospital but who have relatives, neighbors, or acquaintances whom they recognize as taking antipsychotic drugs.

Example
For many years Martin had experienced highs and lows in mood and had been treated with lithium salts, which seemed to control his mood and allow him to function well on the job and with his friends. Martin had a brother, Joe, whose diagnosis was schizophrenia. Joe had been hospitalized several times, had far more disabling symptoms than Martin, was treated with antipsychotics but had never responded very well, had not been able to work for many years, and was a recluse with erratic, embarrassing-to-the-family behavior. As time went by, Martin's own behavior began to deteriorate somewhat, and he began to suffer from delusional thinking and auditory hallucinations. The suggestion that antipsychotic medication could help was, however, immediately and powerfully rejected. Martin could not take the same type of medication as Joe—the potential identification was too humiliating for him.

By the same token, patients previously cooperative with treatment may stop their drugs over the course of time for many of the same reasons that constitute the original resistance. They may experience unpleasant side effects, they may feel well and not wish to be reminded of the time when they were ill, they may find that the drugs simply do not help or else they may stop because of interpersonal difficulties in the doctor-patient relationship. Stopping, by itself, may not be a major problem if it is done with the knowledge of the doctor, and if the doctor-patient relationship continues. It becomes a problem if it is done without the doctor's knowledge or, worse, with the patients' conviction that the doctor will not want to see them drug free, in which case subsequent appointments are missed. While, in some instances, it may be necessary for the doctor to make medication compliance a sine qua non of therapy (for potentially suicidal or violent patients, for instance, who are impossible to treat as outpatients unless they are medicated), it is usually best for the doctor to endure a period of medication rebellion and, by doing so, strengthen the relationship.

Example
Barry, of the previous examples, stopped his medication periodically for a number of reasons: it made him overweight, it reminded him of bad times, it made people think he was crazy, it made him lethargic, and it meant I didn't trust him to be well without it. Invariably, he began to feel worse a few days after stopping. He lost jobs, got into fights with relatives, lost sleep, and was tormented with fears. Although stopping medication usually coincided with an initial decision to stop therapy, the fact that he knew he could always return made phoning for an appointment later (and restarting medications) an easier task.

A difficult issue for young patients is the thought of treatment that has to be continued forever. Older patients become used to the concept of medications that are indefinitely required but for young adults this is a very distressing notion. There are many ways of addressing this worry—one way is to endorse the concept of familiarity with a medication over a brief time period so that in the future, when the illness has abated but threatens to return, another brief course of medications can prevent the development of illness. In case a symptom that is troubling begins to return, it can be quickly dissipated by a known agent, instead of the patient having to repeat the long process of trying out various regimens of different treatments. Part of the difficulty is the issue of not being in control. This is experienced as someone else judging that your behavior is out of line and someone else deciding that you need medication to control it. These fears can be discussed and strategies worked out for self-prescribing—that is, the patient learns which symptoms respond best to medications and takes drugs to combat these symptoms, raising and lowering doses until he or she gets it right. Many patients become adept at this and quite proud that they are able to keep their unpleasant symptoms in check while perhaps permitting other more pleasurable symptoms to occasionally hold sway and compensate them for a life that seems otherwise drab. The quality of life and how it is affected by medications is a crucial issue for the schizophrenic patient (Fenton and McGlashan 1987; Schooler and Levine 1983).

Information About Medication

Patients and families need information about drugs. This can be given in written form, in patient groups, in family groups, in seminars, or one-to-one. Important issues to raise in teaching are grouping symptoms, timing, withdrawal effects, dose effects, side effects, how the drugs work, future drugs, and gender issues.

Grouping symptoms. The antipsychotics work for groups of symptoms, such as those that constitute disorganized behavior (insomnia, hyperactivity, hostility, distractibility, irritability, mood lability, impulsivity) and reality testing (hallucinations, delusions, overvalued ideas, unwarranted fears, feelings of depersonalization). They do not work for the symptoms of psychomotor retardation, withdrawal, apathy, lack of interest, and lack of motivation. Sometimes the antipsychotic medications may make this group of symptoms more severe (Kessler and Waletsky 1981).

Timing. Treatment should usually be started with the lowest possible dose and built up to the limit of tolerance and benefit. Gradual increases prevent side effects. When the decision is made to reduce dosage, this, again, should be done slowly. While there is no set time over which maintenance doses need to be continued, individuals who have suffered psychotic symptoms are at risk for future episodes and need to be warned about prodromal signs so that they can, when necessary, take preventive short courses of drugs periodically, as needed. Some individuals are never free of terrifying psychotic symptoms and for those individuals, drug-free maintenance may be impossible.

Withdrawal effects. Stopping antipsychotics (and the anticholinergics that are often prescribed with them) induces subtle withdrawal effects in many individuals (Dilsaver and Alessi 1988). These effects need to be recognized so that they do not lead to unnecessary restarting of neuroleptics on the assumption that they constitute prodromal signs of psychosis. Gradual stoppage should minimize these effects, which are usually nausea, insomnia, shakiness, headache, and dysphoria.

Dose effects. It is important for patients and families to understand that both beneficial effects and side effects are dose dependent. If a drug does not work, it need not be abandoned; the dose may simply be too low. If a drug produces unpleasant side effects, it need not be discontinued; the dose may need to be reduced. This may be self-evident to doctors but is not to most nonmedical people.

Side effects. All the possible side effects need to be discussed with patients so that they do not get frightened should they experience them. The easiest way to convey the information is by providing a written list and discussing the effects most likely to occur. With very ill individuals this is difficult but can be accomplished with families so that at least they do not become frightened by the unexpected. Oculogyric crises, for instance, are terrifying and the stiffness and tremor secondary to antipsychotic drugs often cause patients and families to feel worse instead of better.

How the drugs work. Most individuals are interested in what exactly the drugs are doing. Although much of this is still not well known, it is useful to go over with patients what is known, to draw simple diagrams, and to demystify the process of chemical-physiological interaction. Most patients are fascinated with how the brain works and short explanations from time to time are welcome, as long as they are not too lengthy and as long as they do not turn the therapeutic interview into a didactic lecture. Essentially, patients need to know that all antipsychotics thus far appear to work by the common pathway of blocking receptors for dopamine at nerve-nerve junctions in the brain, that they all do this at different doses depending on their ability to solubilize in the lipid of the nerve membrane and that different kinds of drugs have different other effects, which determine their side effects or adjunctive effects. A list such as the one appended to this chapter is useful to give to patients and families (see Appendix).

Future drugs. The future is always speculative but I find it necessary to talk to my patients about future drugs, especially to those who do not respond well to those categories of medicines that are available today. It is wise to keep up with new research, not for the purpose of giving patients experimental products but in order to be able to answer their questions and also to offer hope that new, better, more effective, less side-effect-producing drugs are around the corner (Ögren and Högberg 1988).

Example
Sally came to see me with her boyfriend. She was practically mute but the boyfriend told me that she was discouraged by her failure to improve, that all available drugs had been tried, and that nothing seemed to work. I had that morning received a research report about new drugs with great promise that appeared to work through a novel pathway in the brain. The report was well illustrated so I showed Sally the pictures of the new molecules and explained that these were new drugs that were in the testing stage and that were thought to help people like herself who had not responded to the standard dopamine blockers. Sally became visibly interested in the pictures and began to talk about her discouragement and how hard she had tried with, seemingly, no payoff in her ability to cope. Sally and her boyfriend left the office cheered. Since this was a one-time

consultation I do not know for how long this promise of hope helped to lift her mood.

Gender issues. Cyclical hormones in women affect their response to many drugs, including antipsychotics. This is an important issue that merits discussion. Doses may need to be adjusted to meet this changing need. Other gender issues need to be addressed: amenorrhea in women, impotence in men, gynecomastia in men, drugs and pregnancy, drugs during the postpartum period and during lactation, and drugs during menopause (Mitchell and Popkin 1982; Seeman 1984). Since men and women on average show differences in gastric-emptying time, in blood flow to the brain, and in drug lipid storage, doses prescribed to men and women need to be carefully tailored to the needs of each. Gender-specific importance of certain side effects (i.e., obesity, skin problems, muscle stiffness, and tremor) may need to be discussed in the context of what they mean to the patient. Frequently they are also affected by culture, social class, personal expectation, and prior experience (Lin and Finder 1983).

Quality of Life Issue

Doctors sometimes seem to forget that treatments are intended to help the patient feel better, whether or not they eradicate symptoms or produce cures. The concept of cure in psychiatric disease, especially in schizophrenia, is a multidimensional one. The intent of psychiatry is to help patients improve the quality of their life, develop their strengths, minimize their pain, and increase their self-reliance. In schizophrenia, antipsychotic drugs, when well tolerated, can accomplish all these aims. On the other hand, when the drugs are not well tolerated or when patients are resistant to the drugs or nonresponsive to the drugs, continuing to prescribe them without consideration of the patient's concern is destructive to the patient and to the therapeutic relationship. It is possible for schizophrenic patients to enjoy a better quality of life and to be relatively more self-reliant while still experiencing some psychotic symptoms and being relatively free of drugs (Diamond 1985). The measure of success, in other words, is not the patient's compliance to the drug regimen, but rather his or her success in life, which includes management of social relations, leisure time, creativity, satisfaction with housing, a stress-free daily routine—aims that may seem modest but which, for the patient, are often much more important than whether or not psychotic symptoms emerge and whether he or she is gainfully employed or appears to others as mentally well.

Appendix

Information About Antipsychotic Medications for Use as an Educational Tool for Patients and Families

Chlorpromazine. This was the first antipsychotic and continues to be widely used in doses between 100 and 600 mg per day. (Far higher doses are used for hospitalized patients.) CPZ, as it is called, is sedative as well as being antipsychotic because it blocks noradrenaline receptors in the brain to the same extent as it blocks dopamine receptors. This may be beneficial or harmful, depending on patient and circumstance. CPZ results in relatively few neuromuscular side effects (tremors, muscle stiffness, muscle spasms) but, in higher doses, it may lower blood pressure and affect the cardiovascular system. For this reason it is best avoided in the elderly. CPZ does cause skin sensitivity to sunlight more frequently than do other antipsychotics so protection of the skin from sunlight is especially important.

Thioridazine. This drug is used in approximately the same dose range as CPZ. As well as blocking noradrenaline receptors and dopamine receptors, it also has a strong affinity for cholinergic receptors. This means that it almost never induces neuromuscular side effects and is therefore a good drug to use in individuals who are susceptible to these. It may, however, have deleterious effects on the heart, on sexual potency in men, and on the eyes (retinitis pigmentosa), so it should not be a drug of first resort.

Trifluoperazine. This drug is used in doses of 4 to 40 mg per day. Doses are lower than for CPZ because this drug is more fat soluble and is therefore able to enter more easily into the nerve membrane where it exerts its effect. It is less sedative than CPZ but induces more neuromuscular effects. It may therefore require the addition of an anticholinergic drug, at least at the beginning of drug treatment.

Perphenazine. This drug is somewhat similar in potency to trifluoperazine and is used in doses from 4 to 64 mg per day. It is also prone to produce neuromuscular side effects.

Haloperidol. This is a relatively potent drug and may be used in doses from 2 to 40 mg per day. Initially, during an acute psychotic episode, it may be used in higher doses. It is a safe drug with respect to the heart and is therefore used effectively in the elderly and has a large margin of safety when higher-than-average doses are required. It can, however, make the patient stiff, restless, and tremulous and can cause spasms of various muscles. Anticholinergic drugs are usually required to counteract this. Haloperidol is also available as a long-acting depot injection.

Pimozide. This is used in doses of 2 to 24 mg per day and is usually well tolerated with respect to the common side effects of antipsychotics. It is a useful drug for this reason although patients who are more severely ill may not respond.

Fluphenazine. This drug is used in the same dose range as perphenazine and trifluoperazine orally and has the same side effect profile. It also comes in an injectable long-acting form whose effects last for approximately 3 weeks. Fluphenazine is the best known long-acting drug in the United States, although many of the other antipsychotic drugs have long-acting forms that are used in other countries equally effectively. More of these will probably make their way to the United States if their superiority to long-acting fluphenazine is effectively demonstrated.

There are many other forms of antipsychotics currently available in the United States. If one does not seem appropriate, there are many others from which to choose. Newer drugs are being developed and tested. The greatest advance in this area will be drugs with fewer neuromuscular effects and drugs that are effective not only for disorganization and deficient reality testing but also for social withdrawal and lack of motivation. Drugs of this type are being successfully used in Europe and will soon be available internationally.

References

Adelman SA: Pills as transitional objects: a dynamic understanding of the use of medication in psychotherapy. Psychiatry 48:246–253, 1985

Amarasingham LR: Social and cultural perspectives on medication refusal. Am J Psychiatry 137:353–357, 1980

Davis JM: Overview: maintenance therapy in psychiatry, I: schizophrenia. Am J Psychiatry 132:1237–1245, 1975

Diamond R: Drugs and the quality of life: the patient's point of view. J Clin Psychiatry 46:29–35, 1985

Dilsaver SC, Alessi NE: Antipsychotic withdrawal symptoms: phenomenology and pathophysiology. Acta Psychiatr Scand 77:241–246, 1988

Fenton WS, McGlashan TH: Sustained remission in drug-free schizophrenic patients. Am J Psychiatry 144:1306–1309, 1987

Goldhamer PM: Psychotherapy and pharmacotherapy: the

challenge of integration. Can J Psychiatry 28:173–177, 1983

Kessler KA, Waletsky JP: Clinical use of antipsychotics. Am J Psychiatry 138:202–209, 1981

Lin KM, Finder E: Neuroleptic dosage for Asians. Am J Psychiatry 140:490–491, 1983

Mitchell JE, Popkin MK: Antipsychotic drug therapy and sexual dysfunction in men. Am J Psychiatry 139:633–637, 1982

Ögren SO, Högberg T: Novel dopamine D-2 antagonists for the treatment of schizophrenia. ISI Atlas of Science: Pharmacology 2:141–146, 1988

Schooler NR, Levine J: Strategies for enhancing drug therapy of schizophrenia. Am J Psychother 37:521–532, 1983

Seeman MV: Pharmacological features and the effects of neuroleptics. Can Med Assoc J 125:821–826, 1981

Seeman MV: Neuroleptic response: predictive clinical clues. Ayd International Drug Therapy Newsletter 19(1), 1984

Tupin JP: Focal neuroleptization: an approach to optimal dosing for initial and continuing therapy. J Clin Psychopharmacol 5 (suppl 3):155–215, 1985

Van Putten T: Why do schizophrenic patients refuse their drugs? Arch Gen Psychiatry 31:67–72, 1974

Chapter 8

Adjunct Therapies

PETER BROWN, M.D., F.R.C.P.(C)

Chapter 8

Adjunct Therapies

*T*he goal of this chapter is to outline new approaches to the diagnosis and management of some of the more common difficulties of the schizophrenic patient. While symptoms such as delusions, hallucinations, or thought disorder may be the more spectacular manifestations of schizophrenia, the clinician treating a schizophrenic patient is often called upon to help with a number of more mundane but no less important problems of this chronic and pervasive brain disorder. The list includes mood disturbances, particularly anxiety and depression, and the psychological and physiologic effects of long-term medication use (Table 1). What is more, these problems are often directly related to the severity of unresolved psychotic symptoms. Dealing properly with these key issues can have a substantial impact on both the quality of life for the patient and on the quality of the therapeutic relationship.

Mood Disturbance and Extrapyramidal Syndromes

Anxiety and depression are the most common symptoms of schizophrenia. Moreover, these are among the symptoms for which clinicians have the most effective psychologic and pharmacologic treatments in all of psychiatry. However, this situation is complicated by the fact that these features must be differentiated from the two most common side effects of neuroleptic medication: akathisia and akinesia. Thus, the first step

Table 1. Adjunctive drug treatments

Parkinsonism and akathisia
  Amantadine
  Beta blockers
  Clonidine
  Iron; calcium
Mood disorders
  Tricyclic antidepressants
  Benzodiazepines (e.g., alprazolam)
Endocrine and sexual dysfunction
  Bromocriptine
  Amantadine
Psychotic symptoms
  Lithium
  Carbamazepine

in dealing with anxiety and depression in schizophrenic patients is to rule out neuroleptic-induced syndromes.

It is not surprising that these syndromes may be difficult to differentiate. Affective disturbances and extrapyramidal syndromes are characterized by similar cognitive, emotional, and behavioral manifestations. In addition, there may be considerable overlap. Significant depression is found in a substantial number of patients with parkinsonism, while anxiety is frequent in those patients with akathisia. It is this degree of overlap that accounts for much of the continued difficulty that clinicians have in identifying neuroleptic-induced syndromes, despite decades of experience with their use. For example, a recent series suggested that less than one-third of psychotic patients with akathisia are correctly identified (Weiden et al. 1987).

Akathisia and Anxiety

Akathisia was originally described as part of the early manifestations of Parkinson's disease (Sacks 1983). Today, the syndrome is most commonly seen secondary to neuroleptic administration. Although estimates vary widely, the commonly accepted prevalence figures reported are in the area of

20% (Van Putten 1975). The syndrome typically occurs within 40 days of a change of neuroleptic dosage and is slightly more common in women and in the elderly (Ratey and Salzman 1984; Steinberg 1985; Van Putten 1975).

Akathisia is a strong and extremely unpleasant sensation of being unable to control motor behavior. Patients may describe themselves as feeling restless, out of control, or compelled to move. The sensation is most often experienced in the limbs or in the abdomen (Braude et al. 1984; Sacks 1983). Associated with these subjective experiences are repetitive motor movements including leg crossing, leg swinging, outward rotation of the leg, foot tapping, hand wringing, and rapid walking (Braude et al. 1984; Gibb and Lees 1986). The overall experience, both for the patient and for an observer, is one of extreme psychic agitation. With these varied forms of presentation, it is essential to recognize that the disorder consists of two symptom complexes: one sensory and the other motor (Brown 1988).

These symptoms may result in akathisia being mistaken for a variety of psychiatric disorders, including agitated depression and psychotic decompensation, as well as primary anxiety (Van Putten 1975). Thus, "agitated" patients should always be carefully assessed for akathisia before increases in neuroleptic medication are prescribed. Misinterpretation of the symptoms can lead to a dramatically escalating cycle of increased akathisia and increased doses of neuroleptic. Akathisia is an extremely distressing symptom that, if misdiagnosed and left untreated, can have considerable impact on the course of treatment. As well as the personal distress, akathisia can also result in noncompliance with medication and a general deterioration of the rapport between patient and physician. Furthermore, if left unchecked, the distress produced by akathisia may even lead to explosive violence or suicide (Drake and Ehrlich 1985; Keckich 1978; Shear et al. 1983).

Akathisia can be more easily identified if associated features are noted (Table 2). In addition to their subjective distress and motor symptoms, patients typically demonstrate

---

Table 2. Signs and symptoms of akathisia

Complaints
  Restlessness, tension, jitters, butterflies, or "feeling out of control," especially in the limbs or abdomen
Motor features
  Repeated leg crossing, leg swinging, outward rotation of the leg, foot tapping, hand wringing, or rapid walking
Associated features of mild parkinsonism
  Blank or diminished facial expression, shuffling gait, lack of accessory movements of upper limbs, cogwheel rigidity (elicited by recruitment), diminished blink rate, and failure of the glabellar reflex to habituate

---

other evidence of mild or early extrapyramidal dysfunction such as decreases in facial expression (despite complaints of extreme subjective distress), a rapid shuffling gait with a lack of accessory movements, decreased blink rate, and a positive glabellar reflex (Brown 1988). A mild intention tremor and cogwheel rigidity are frequently present. Mild rigidity can best be elicited by recruitment (Maltbie and Cavenar 1977). Standardized interview and examination procedures can also considerably increase the diagnostic accuracy (Chouinard et al. 1979; Munetz and Benjamin 1988).

In addition, there is some preliminary evidence that laboratory tests may assist in making the diagnosis. Braude and co-workers (1984) were able to distinguish akathisic patients from controls using electromyographic techniques. Patients were characterized by the presence of large amplitude, low frequency (less than 4 Hz), rhythmic foot movements. This is the first report of a potentially useful diagnostic tool in this disorder. More recently, K. Brown and co-workers (1987) reported decreased serum iron and percentage iron saturation, and increased total iron binding capacity in the blood of patients with akathisia when compared with controls.

The clinical lore is that akathisia is often difficult to manage. The standard approach consists of reduction of the dose of the offending agent and treatment with one of a variety of antiparkinsonian medications (Ratey and Salzman 1984). However, clinicians are often reluctant to attempt reductions of neuroleptic medication, particularly at a time when the patient may be extremely agitated and showing features of psychotic decompensation. However, it should be recalled that the distress caused by akathisia may in fact be an important precipitant in exacerbating psychotic features. Adequate treatment of akathisia may result in a simultaneous decrease in psychotic symptoms (i.e., in enhanced clinical response to the neuroleptic medications) (Cohen 1987).

Currently there are a wide number of agents that are effective for some patients. Antiparkinsonian agents, benzodiazepines, beta blockers, and clonidine have all been reported to be effective in reducing symptoms (Chouinard et al. 1979; Cohen 1987; Donlon 1973; Dupuis et al. 1987; Gagrat et al. 1978; Lipinski et al. 1984; Ratey and Salzman 1984; Ratey et al. 1985; Zubenko et al. 1984). Propranolol has been reported to be superior to benztropine in a single open trial (Adler et al. 1986b). Controlled trials of propranolol and clonidine have also been reported to provide significant overall improvement (Adler et al. 1986a, 1987). There is also a suggestion that concurrent administration of iron may be of benefit for some patients (Brown et al. 1987).

What is lacking is a way of identifying which of these treatments will most benefit a particular patient. In the absence of definitive research, the individual clinician is left with no specific, clear guidelines as to which of these agents is to be preferred. That decision will require a consideration of the benefits and drawbacks of each medication (for example, avoiding benzodiazepines with patients who are likely to abuse them, and avoiding beta blockers in certain patients with significant concomitant medical illnesses).

If akathisia has been ruled out, the clinician can address the management of anxiety. It should be recalled that neuroleptics are relatively poor anxiolytics. Alprazolam and other benzodiazepines can be effective in the symptomatic reduction of anxiety symptoms, as well as in the treatment of akathisia. The addition of alprazolam in the range of 2–4 mg per day has been reported to be of significant value in reducing anxiety as well as both positive and negative psychotic symptoms in schizophrenic patients (Wolkowitz et al. 1986). The mechanism of action is not completely clear. Benzodiazepines may work directly on psychotic symptoms, or indirectly by either the relief of affective symptoms, particularly anxiety, or by control of akathisia (Lipinski and Cohen 1986).

Schizophrenic patients with panic attacks have been reported to respond favorably when alprazolam was added to neuroleptic medication (Kahn et al. 1988). Improvement occurred not only in panic symptoms but also in both the positive and the negative symptoms of schizophrenia. Doses of alprazolam ranged from 0.5 to 0.75 mg, qid.

Depression and Akinesia

Depression is common in schizophrenic patients. Depression, however, is frequently overlooked or interpreted as evidence of the negative symptoms of schizophrenia. Approximately one-half of the patients who meet criteria for depression in schizophrenia will also satisfy protocol criteria for negative symptoms (Siris et al. 1988). Flat affect, lack of energy, and loss of motivation can be the result of drug-induced parkinsonism or depression as well as a part of the deficit state found in schizophrenia. There is often a reluctance to treat "subclinical" or relatively mild forms of extrapyramidal disorders. However, current research reveals substantial cognitive and emotional dysfunction associated with this level of the disorder (Brown 1988). Thus patients with features of extrapyramidal symptoms should be treated even if the physical findings are relatively mild.

The standard treatment of akinesia or parkinsonism is covered in Chapter 10. In addition to standard antiparkinsonian medications, newer agents such as amantadine can be highly effective. Patients who fail to respond with agents such as benztropine or who are troubled by anticholinergic side effects can be tried on 200–300 mg of amantadine daily

(McEvoy et al. 1987a). Also, amantadine does not show evidence of the negative effects on memory that the other antiparkinsonian medications may produce in some elderly patients (McEvoy et al. 1987b).

Surveys comparing current approaches with those of the last decade suggest that parkinsonism is being better treated in chronic schizophrenic patients through a combination of generally lower doses of neuroleptic medication and more frequent use of prophylactic antiparkinsonian medication (Gelenberg 1987). It is important to note that prophylactic antiparkinsonian drug therapy may not only significantly improve motor function but also reduce many symptoms of psychopathology (Jellinek et al. 1981; Manos et al. 1981).

Calcium has also been reported as being of possible benefit in neuroleptic-induced extrapyramidal reactions, and patients with hypocalcemia may be at greater risk for these types of drug-related syndromes (Fernando and Manchanda 1988).

Generally speaking, effectively dealing with neuroleptic side effects can also produce improvement in the symptoms of schizophrenia. This may simply be the result of eliminating an unpleasant physical and emotional experience or there may be a direct effect on the illness process. Nevertheless, it should be underlined that it is also clear that not all patients respond in a similar fashion and antiparkinsonian medication can be associated in some cases with worsening of the clinical state (Nestelbaum et al. 1986). Such worsening may be the result of antiparkinsonian toxicity. The state of our clinical knowledge simply does not allow for a generalization for all schizophrenic patients.

It is also important to deal with features of depression. Clinically, evidence of depression should always be sought when assessing negative symptoms. Recent evidence would suggest that depression can be differentiated from deficit symptoms in chronic schizophrenia with careful clinical assessment (Whiteford et al. 1987). Similarly, in a well-designed randomized double-blind trial, Siris and co-workers (1988) demonstrated that schizophrenic patients with depressive features and "negative symptoms" respond equally well to standard antidepressant treatment.

In conclusion, many patients with schizophrenia have significant cognitive, affective, and behavioral symptoms of anxiety and depression. The first task of the clinician in an office setting is to rule out the possibility that these features are secondary to neuroleptic use (either akathisia or akinesia). Similarly, the clinician should be aware of anxiety and affective disorders rather than assuming that such symptoms are the result of "psychotic agitation" or "negative symptoms." Anxiety, depression, and extrapyramidal syndromes will generally respond to the appropriate measures provided they are correctly identified. Effective management of such disorders can make a significant improvement in the quality of the patient's life as well as in enhancing the rapport between physician and patient. The development of a positive therapeutic relationship can be considerably strengthened by sympathetic attention to these features of the disorder and its treatment, and by their effective management.

Insomnia

Acute insomnia is a frequent symptom of schizophrenia often secondary to psychotic exacerbation, depression, anxiety, akathisia, or concurrent medical disorders. Management always involves reassurance and treatment of the underlying disorder. Chronic insomnia is generally the result of either poor sleep hygiene or sleep fragmentation secondary to prolonged dependence on hypnotic medication. Management involves 1) establishment of a regular circadian rhythm of activities; 2) application of sleep hygiene procedures (regular bedtime, mild exercise, decreased caffeine intake in second half of day); and 3) a gradual reduction of hypnotic dependency. With the cooperation of patient and family these steps are effective in the majority of cases.

Neuroleptic-Induced Endocrine and Sexual Dysfunction

The neuroleptics' dopamine blocking effects also produce increased levels of prolactin in the blood. Neuroleptic-induced hyperprolactinemia may result in a number of endocrine effects such as galactorrhea, weight gain, breast tenderness, and amenorrhea in females, and gynecomastia and decreases in sexual function or desire in males. In males, these complaints are typically associated with lowered testosterone levels. The dopamine agonist bromocriptine has been reported to reverse amenorrhea and decrease lactation in female patients while increasing serum testosterone levels and improving sexual desire and function (Matsuoka et al. 1986). None of the patients who were in this small open trial experienced a worsening of their psychotic symptoms. Full response to bromocriptine may take several months.

Similarly, in an open trial, Correa and co-workers (1987) reported a significant reduction of endocrine and sexual symptoms with doses of 200–300 mg of amantadine daily for periods of 2–3 weeks. Significantly, these workers also reported a significant decrease in overall psychiatric symptoms while the neuroendocrine symptoms were being treated. This finding underlines the notion that control of psychotic symptoms and side effects are not necessarily mutually exclusive.

Adjunctive or Alternative Treatment of Psychotic Symptoms

While the neuroleptics remain the mainstays of antipsychotic treatment, two other agents merit comment. Carbamazepine may be of use in some patients who are unresponsive to neuroleptic medication. While further systematic studies are required, carbamazepine in doses between 300 and 1200 mg per day may be effective for some patients (Neppe 1988). In a clinical trial with 12 schizophrenic patients nonresponsive to treatment, 4 of 12 patients improved significantly, while a worsening was observed in 8 (Sramek et al. 1988). The doses used in this study ranged between 400 and 600 mg per day. Thus, carbamazepine may be of value in some treatment-resistant schizophrenic patients but further studies are required. However, while carbamazepine is well tolerated by most patients, hepatic, renal, and hematologic complications have been described. Physicians must carefully monitor basic hematologic and biochemical functions on a weekly basis for the first 6 months of treatment and monthly thereafter. Carbamazepine serum levels, while accurate, have as yet little clinical value in either establishing a therapeutic range or in alerting against possible toxicity. Carbamazepine withdrawal may also exacerbate some patients' illnesses so that when a trial of carbamazepine is terminated, the drug should be tapered off very gradually (Heh et al. 1988). Thus, while promising, this agent has yet to be clearly characterized with regard to its value in schizophrenia, either alone or in combination with other agents.

There is a growing awareness of the value of lithium treatment in schizophrenia and schizoaffective disorders. It has become progressively clearer that the benefits of lithium are not limited to the classic bipolar patients (Delva and Letemendia 1982; Hirschowitz et al. 1980; Sautter and Garver 1985). It is likely that the use of lithium in schizophrenic patients will continue to become more frequent over the next few years. Lithium's use may be of value in reducing the frequency of secondary affective syndromes as well as dealing with the primary features of schizophrenia. In addition, lithium may be of benefit in reducing tardive syndromes both by providing a direct protection from long-term neuroleptic effects as well as possibly reducing neuroleptic dosage requirements. Currently, lithium represents the single most important and potentially useful adjunct to our conventional treatment of schizophrenia of all of the other alternates that have been proposed.

A continuing advance has been made in the area of individualized drug dosages. The scarcity of viable alternatives and the frequency of relative or absolute lack of response (as well as the frequency of tardive syndromes) has led to a reexamination of traditional drug regimens. Recent evidence suggests the value of a flexible, targeted approach to neuroleptic administration plus psychosocial intervention for a significant number of schizophrenic patients. Patients in an open trial who were treated in this manner did at least as well as control group patients in more conventional treatment, despite receiving considerably less medication (Carpenter et al. 1987). Our approach must remain flexible. While some patients will significantly benefit from a reduction in neuroleptic dosage, both positive and negative symptoms of other patients can be significantly reduced by increased neuroleptic treatment in other patients. Similarly, the dosage requirements of any particular patient will vary over time (Breier et al. 1987).

In conclusion, the bulk of the evidence would suggest that there is no single uniform pharmacologic strategy for dealing with all schizophrenic patients just as there is no single strategy for insulin requirements for all diabetic patients. Dosages must be individualized for each patient. Continuous standard dose, continuous low dose, and targeted specific symptom treatment are all effective for some patients. Similarly, both oral and depot medications have specific advantages, but a flexibility in approach is clearly the most effective way of ensuring effective treatment (Carpenter et al. 1987).

Tardive Syndromes

Tardive dyskinesia, tardive dystonia, and other types of oral or facial neuromuscular disorders have all been described following prolonged use of neuroleptic medication (Ananth et al. 1988). Prolonged neurologic syndromes secondary to psychotropic medication such as tardive dyskinesia have been estimated to have a prevalence of between 1 and 50%. More recent rigorous studies suggest that the incidence may be between 3 and 4% (Yagi and Itoh 1985; Chouinard et al. 1986; Gelenberg 1987). Given the lack of successful clinical treatment for severe dyskinesia and other tardive syndromes, the most profitable approach for the clinician is to try to avoid it as much as possible in the first place. This involves a conservative use of antipsychotic medication, both with regard to the duration of treatment and the dosage. Recent studies suggest that a significant number of schizophrenic patients may do very well with intermittent drug therapy at relatively low doses (Carpenter et al. 1987). Patients with a history of severe parkinsonian reactions appear also to be at greater risk for the development of tardive syndromes (Chouinard et al. 1986). Thus, patients who have a minimal therapeutic response to neuroleptics or who experience severe intractable side effects should be treated by other methods.

Other Therapies

All too frequently, psychiatric clinicians are biased by their training to limit their approaches to the treatment of schizophrenic patients to medication and psychotherapy. However, it has become increasingly clear that other treatment approaches are of significant value when used in adjunct with the mainstay approaches. It is no more appropriate to treat a schizophrenic patient with medication and psychotherapy alone than it is to treat a diabetic patient with medication and psychotherapy alone. For example, regular, well-balanced meals provide not only good nutrition but a powerful zeitgeber can enhance social function. Diet, exercise programs, and social and community interventions are necessary for every patient with a major chronic illness.

Behavioral approaches to schizophrenia have been effective but largely limited to inpatient treatment. Such programs can be extremely useful if the reinforcement schedules can be tied to real-life events for outpatient treatment. It would appear that a relative lack of expertise with behavioral approaches is responsible for the relative lack of this type of treatment. Behavioral techniques are easily integrated with other therapies and have beneficial effects beyond their target symptoms. Behavioral approaches such as social skills training have been shown to be effective not only in improving social function but in decreasing overall levels of symptomatology and preventing hospitalization (Liberman et al. 1986). These findings underline the necessity for a comprehensive approach with a multidisciplined health care team in the treatment of schizophrenia just as much as in any chronic illness (for a review, see Liberman 1985).

Conclusion

Overall there appear to be a number of trends in contemporary treatment of schizophrenic patients:

1. A heightened awareness of extrapyramidal syndromes and a more aggressive approach in their management.
2. An increased clinical sensitivity to symptoms of depression and anxiety in schizophrenic patients, and more aggressive management of depression and anxiety with antidepressants and benzodiazepines.
3. A trend toward more flexible individualized doses of neuroleptic medication in general and toward flexible dosage systems, drug holidays, and individualized approaches in particular;
4. A continued increase in the frequency of adding lithium carbonate to neuroleptic medication in patients whose symptoms are not adequately controlled.
5. The continued lack of a true alternative to neuroleptic medication as the mainstay in the treatment of schizophrenia.

Our continued desire for a definitive cure for schizophrenia should not obscure our growing ability to substantially improve the care of many patients with existing techniques. While there is no "magic bullet" for schizophrenia, the past decade has seen significant progress in the tailoring of treatment for the individual patient. Advances in knowledge have made it possible to be more sensitive to individual needs, thereby enhancing the collaborative aspect of treatment. This is the heart of the therapeutic alliance for any chronic illness, with both physician and patient making an active contribution.

References

Adler L, Angrist B, Peselow E, et al: A controlled assessment of propranolol in the treatment of neuroleptic-induced akathisa. Br J Psychiatry 149:42–45, 1986a

Adler L, Reitano J, Corwin J, et al: Differential effects of propranolol and benztropine (poster). Presented at the annual meeting of American College of Neuropsychopharmacology, Washington, DC, May 6–11, 1986b

Adler LA, Angrist B, Peselow E, et al: Clonidine in neuroleptic-induced akathisia. Am J Psychiatry 144:235–236, 1987

Ananth J, Edelmuth E, Dargan B: Meige's syndrome associated with neuroleptic treatment. Am J Psychiatry 145:513–515, 1988

Braude WM, Charles IP, Barnes TRE: Coarse, jerky foot tremor: tremographic investigation of an objective sign of acute akathisia. Psychopharmacology 82:95–101, 1984

Breier A, Wolkowitz OM, Doran AR, et al: Neuroleptic responsivity of negative and positive symptoms in schizophrenia. Am J Psychiatry 144:1549–1555, 1987

Brown KW, Glen SE, White T: Low serum iron status and akathisia. Lancet 1:1234–1236, 1987

Brown P: Review: Drug induced akathisia in medical and surgical patients. Int J Psychiatry Med 181:1–15, 1988

Carpenter WT Jr, Heinrichs DW, Hanlon TE: A comparative trial of pharmacologic strategies in schizophrenia. Am J Psychiatry 144:1466–1470, 1987

Chouinard G, Annable L, Ross-Chouinard A, et al: Ethopropazine and benztropine in neuroleptic-induced parkinsonism. J Clin Psychiatry 40:147–152, 1979

Chouinard G, Annable L, Mercier P: A five-year follow-up study of tardive dyskinesia. Psychopharmacol Bull 22:259–263, 1986

Cohen BM: Akathisia: treatment and pathophysiology. Chicago, APA Abstracts 96, 1987

Correa N, Opler LA, Kay SR, et al: Amantadine in the treatment of neuroendocrine side effects. J Clin Psychopharmacol 7:91–95, 1987

Delva NJ, Letemendia FJJ: Lithium treatment in schizophrenia and schizo-affective disorder. Br J Psychiatry 141:387–400, 1982

Donlon PT: The therapeutic use of diazepam for akathisia. Psychosomatics 14:222–225, 1973

Drake RE, Ehrlich J: Suicide attempts associated with akathisia. Am J Psychiatry 142:499–501, 1985

Dupuis B, Catteau J, Dumon J-P, et al: Comparison of propranolol, sotalol, and betaxolol in the treatment of neuroleptic-induced akathisia. Am J Psychiatry 144:802–805, 1987

Fernando MLD, Manchanda R: Calcium therapy for neuroleptic-induced extrapyramidal symptoms (letter). Br J Psychiatry 152:722–723, 1988

Gagrat D, Hamilton J, Belmaker RH: Intravenous diazepam in the treatment of neuroleptic-induced acute dystonia and akathisia. Am J Psychiatry 135:1232–1233, 1978

Gelenberg, AJ: Treating extrapyramidal reactions: some current issues. J Clin Psychiatry 48 (suppl):24–27, 1987

Gibb WRG, Lees AJ: The clinical phenomenon of akathisia. J Neurol Neurosurg Psychiatry 49:861–866, 1986

Heh CWC, Sramek J, Herrera J, et al: Exacerbation of psychosis after discontinuation of carbamazepine treatment. Am J Psychiatry 145:878–879, 1988

Hirschowitz J, Casper R, Garver DL, et al: Lithium response in good prognosis schizophrenia. Am J Psychiatry 137:916–920, 1980

Jellinek T, Gardos G, Cole JO: Adverse effects of antiparkinson drug withdrawal. Am J Psychiatry 138:1567–1571, 1981

Kahn JP, Puertollano MA, Schane MD, et al: Adjunctive

alprazolam for schizophrenia with panic anxiety: clinical observation and pathogenetic implications. Am J Psychiatry 145:742–744, 1988

Keckich WA: Neuroleptics: violence as a manifestation of akathisia (letter). JAMA 240:2185, 1978

Liberman RP: Schizophrenia: psychosocial treatment, in Comprehensive Textbook of Psychiatry/IV, 4th Ed. Edited by Kaplan HI, Sadock BJ. Baltimore, Williams & Wilkins, 1985, pp 724–734

Liberman RP, Mueser, KT, Wallace CJ: Social skills training for schizophrenic individuals at risk for relapse. Am J Psychiatry 143:523–526, 1986

Lipinski JF Jr, Cohen BM: Alprazolam-neuroleptic combination in schizophrenia (letter). Am J Psychiatry 143:1501, 1986

Lipinski JF Jr, Zubenko GS, Cohen BM, et al: Propranolol in the treatment of neuroleptic-induced akathisia. Am J Psychiatry 141:412–415, 1984

Maltbie AA, Cavenar JO Jr: Akathisia diagnosis: an objective test. Psychosomatics 18:36–39, 1977

Manos N, Gkiouzepas J, Logothetis J: The need for continuous use of antiparkinsonian medication with chronic schizophrenic patients receiving long-term neuroleptic therapy. Am J Psychiatry 138:184–188, 1981

Matsuoka I, Nakai T, Miyake M, et al: Effects of bromocriptine on neuroleptic-induced amenorrhea, galactorrhea and impotence. Jpn J Psychiatry Neurol 40:639–646, 1986

McEvoy JP, McCue M, Freter S: Replacement of chronically administered anticholinergic drugs by amantadine in outpatient management of chronic schizophrenia. Clin Ther 9:429–433, 1987a

McEvoy JP, McCue M, Spring B, et al: Effects of amantadine and trihexyphenidyl on memory in elderly normal volunteers. Am J Psychiatry 144:573–577, 1987b

Munetz MR, Benjamin S: How to examine patients using the abnormal involuntary movement scale. Hosp Community Psychiatry 39:1172–1177, 1988

Neppe VM: Carbamazepine in nonresponsive psychosis. J Clin Psychiatry 49 (April suppl):22–28, 1988

Nestelbaum Z, Siris SG, Rifkin A, et al: Exacerbation of schizophrenia associated with amantadine. Am J Psychiatry 143:1170–1171, 1986

Ratey JJ, Salzman C: Recognizing and managing akathisia. Hosp Community Psychiatry 35:975–977, 1984

Ratey JJ, Sorgi P, Polakoff S: Nadolol as a treatment for akathisia. Am J Psychiatry 142:640–642, 1985

Sacks O: Awakenings. New York, Dutton, 1983

Sautter F, Garver D: Familial differences in lithium responsive versus lithium nonresponsive psychoses. J Psychiatr Res 19:1–8, 1985

Shear MK, Frances A, Weiden P: Suicide associated with akathisia and depot fluphenazine treatment. J Clin Psychopharmacol 3:235–236, 1983

Siris SG, Adan F, Cohen M, et al: Postpsychotic depression and negative symptoms: an investigation of syndromal overlap. Am J Psychiatry 145:1532–1537, 1988

Sramek J, Herrera J, Costa J, et al: A carbamazepine trial in chronic, treatment-refractory schizophrenia. Am J Psychiatry 145:748–750, 1988

Steinberg SK: Drug-induced extrapyramidal symptoms in the elderly. Modern Medicine of Canada 40:473–482, 1985

Van Putten T: The many faces of akathisia. Compr Psychiatry 16:43–47, 1975

Weiden PJ, Mann JJ, Haas G, et al: Clinical nonrecognition of neuroleptic-induced movement disorders: a cautionary study. Am J Psychiatry 144:1148–1153, 1987

Whiteford HA, Riney SJ, Csernansky JG: Distinguishing depressive and negative symptoms in chronic schizophrenia. Psychopathology 20:234–236, 1987

Wolkowitz OM, Pickar D, Doran AR, et al: Combination alprazolam-neuroleptic treatment of the positive and negative symptoms of schizophrenia. Am J Psychiatry 143:85–87, 1986

Yagi G, Itoh H: A ten-year follow-up study of tardive dyskinesia—with special reference to the influence of neuroleptic administration on the long-term prognosis. Keio J Med 34:211–219, 1985

Zubenko GS, Cohen BM, Lipinski JF Jr, et al: Use of clonidine in treating neuroleptic-induced akathisia. Psychiatry Res 13:253–259, 1984

Chapter 9

Networking

PAUL GOLDHAMER, M.D., F.R.C.P.(C)

Chapter 9

Networking

The treatment of a schizophrenic patient has become a multi-disciplinary enterprise. A patient may receive help from several of the following: nurse, family doctor, psychiatrist, psychologist, rehabilitation worker, case manager, occupational therapist, social worker, discharge planner, and art (or music or drama or recreation) therapist. This multiplicity of approaches and treaters provides several advantages. Therapists from different disciplines provide additional and complementary perspectives. The patient is obliged to be involved with more people, increasing his or her contacts in the world and lessening isolation. An excessively dependent attachment to one person is prevented.

In addition to therapeutic relationships, a patient will typically be involved with many government and social agencies that are trying to promote his or her welfare. How does the patient survive so many helpers, especially when they often pursue contradictory goals?

Example
Kent, a 26-year-old single man, has been receiving a government disability pension. He has had six psychotic episodes. In each he has become manic and spent money extravagantly including savings and an inheritance. He now lives at home with his family and is able to save a portion of each check, with the goal of having enough savings to live on his own. I have expressed my satisfaction to him about his increased sense of responsibility and thrift. I became worried when he again spoke

of expensive purchases. When I inquired about the behavior, he explained that his disability worker had advised him to spend his money more liberally (and even provided suggestions, e.g., cameras, VCRs) to avoid reaching too high a bank balance.

The Case Management Model

When patients lived in asylums for years, all their needs were met in one institution. Now patients are hospitalized briefly and sent back to the community. However, they are often ill-equipped to handle residential, vocational, recreational, social, and financial needs. In order to ensure that patients' various needs are met and that care is not fragmented, uncoordinated, or even contradictory, the case management model was developed. One individual was to maintain a continuing responsibility to monitor that the patient was receiving all the care and services that he or she required and was entitled to (Intagliata 1982).

Lamb (1982) has suggested that this case manager be the patient's primary therapist, that is, a person clinically involved with the patient rather than an administrator. The case manager/therapist can then evaluate the clinical effects of the many experiences in the life of the patient. I would suggest that it is even more desirable for a physician (family doctor or psychiatrist) to perform many of these case management functions. The physician is most knowledgeable about the patient's medical and psychiatric status and can enhance his or her understanding of the patient by more thoroughly familiarizing himself or herself with all facets of the patient's life. The more the physician can learn about a patient's various life experiences, the better able he or she is to assess and treat that patient. As the patient recognizes that the doctor is truly interested and committed to improving his or her quality of life, the patient may tend to be more accepting of medical interventions. Also, community agencies are often more receptive to the intervention and advice of a physician than to the advice of nonmedical staff.

Example
Jane is a 40-year-old single schizophrenic woman. She has a chronically delusional belief that the mayor is secretly in love with her and that he tortures her with his advances. She has refused medication but comes for appointments urging me to assist her in receiving compensation from the mayor. I have explained that I cannot aid her in that way. However, I have helped her receive other financial services to which she is entitled, that is, a subsidized apartment, a disability pension, and relief from having to pay interest on a student loan. After I was able to help her achieve greater financial security, she accepted medication from me, and the intensity of her delusional ideas has abated.

A patient's needs can be categorized into medical psychiatric services, housing, social recreational, vocational and educational, other therapy, and rehabilitation (Wasylenki et al. 1986). In order to help a patient achieve satisfaction in these areas, the physician must be familiar with the patient's abilities and disabilities and desires through a thorough assessment (Chapter 2). The clinician must also be aware of the resources in the community that can serve the patient's needs.

Medical Psychiatric Services

The psychiatrist must ensure that the patient is receiving adequate medical care. Schizophrenic patients may be reluctant to undergo medical examinations, but regular check-ups and tests are necessary, because patients are generally receiving potent medication and they do have a higher-than-average incidence of physical illness (Wasylenki et al. 1986). Farmer (1987) found that more than one-half of a sample of chronic psychiatric patients in a community program had undiagnosed physical health problems. More than one-third had known medical problems that warranted more evaluation or additional treatment.

Patients will at times require emergency services for medical or psychiatric problems and occasionally need brief rehospitalizations (Chapter 10). It is important for the primary psychiatrist to have contact with other medical practitioners, to improve the patient's compliance with medical services, and to help foster positive relationships between other physicians and the psychiatric patient.

Example
Robert is a 35-year-old schizophrenic man who has had over 20 psychiatric admissions in the past 12 years and has required frequent medical care. He has been proud of his decreasing need for emergency psychiatric services in the past year. One evening he went to the emergency room of his regular hospital because of acute abdominal pain. He was received at the emergency room with the statement from one physician to another, "Robert is a well-known psychiatric patient who comes here frequently." He felt insulted and humiliated and was further enraged by the lack of careful consideration to his medical complaints.

Emergency staff are frequently overworked and may dismiss psychiatric patients as "crocks." The psychiatrist can perform an especially valuable service by providing liaison and education to the nurses and physicians in the emergency ward.

Housing

Satisfactory housing is an essential factor contributing to the quality of anyone's life, no less the schizophrenic patient. If the patient lives with his or her family, providing support and education for the family is vital (Chapter 6). If the patient lives on his or her own, it can often be very difficult to find affordable housing that meets the patient's needs. The housing should provide the support and structure that is necessary, without being too restrictive. A variety of alternatives is necessary, including short-term emergency facilities, group homes, independent apartments, and very structured environments for the most chronically disabled (Meyerson and Herman 1983; Talbott 1984). In all instances, residential staff or landlords require assistance in the form of education and consultation.

Example
Robert lives in an excellent group home with a low staff-to-resident ratio and a dedicated staff. Nevertheless, Robert occasionally infuriates and worries the staff with his incessant conversation about his delusions, for example, that he is the Antichrist, that the world will soon end according to the messages he has directly received from God, and that he has had many supernatural experiences. He is offended if his claims to special powers are contradicted. I discussed with the staff at his residence the difficulties he presents to them and to other clients. Staff members were concerned that he seemed psychotic and required more medication and that his conversation was upsetting to other residents. I suggested that he was well medicated but continued to talk about his delusions as he appreciated the special attention they elicited and had a very high need and liking of attention and admiration. We agreed on a plan of action. He would come to our clinic twice a week to meet with his nurse therapist, and once to meet with me. At the residence, he would be limited to 20 minutes a day in which he could talk to staff but not other residents about his supernatural powers. Staff would listen and not contradict these ideas. At other times he would be particularly praised when he was attracting attention in a more acceptable manner, for example, playing the piano, which he enjoyed and was proficient at.

Sometimes well-intentioned staff or landlords can be too tolerant of psychiatric patients. A patient's abusive or destructive behavior will be permitted, because it is thought that the patient cannot control his or her behavior. The consulting psychiatrist can reassure residential staff that limit setting is not only acceptable but desirable. In other instances the residential staff may have excessive expectations for a resident, and the consultant can help the staff develop realistic expectations and

167

phase in appropriate goals for the resident. A consultant can also be helpful in aiding the residence staff in their selection of suitable residents.

Example
An agency was seeking a placement for Susan, a quiet, pleasant 30-year-old single schizophrenic woman. The agency wanted to recommend her to a co-op residence, where she would share a room with two or three other women, and also share household chores. As Susan was eager to leave home, she readily agreed. However, I was aware that Susan was very prone to becoming paranoid, if she lived or worked too closely with other women, and I recommended a more private, less intrusive setting for her. When asked which she preferred, she agreed that she would like a private room, but was disappointed at having to wait.

Social and Recreational Services

A patient may satisfy his or her own social recreational needs but more often requires guidance by his or her therapist. Too many patients lead an isolated, understimulating life with little opportunity for social interactions. Occasionally a patient tries too hard to maintain a busy social life, and moves frantically from one activity to another, desperately trying to fit in. The clinician who is aware of a patient's social skills and requirements can guide the patient in avoiding under- or overstimulation. The physician is not likely to be familiar with the variety of community activities but should be able to refer the patient to a community worker or occupational or recreational therapist who is. Community activities that a patient may participate in will include mainstream activities available to all, for example in community centers, libraries, or colleges. Participating in programs not designed for psychiatric patients helps the patient avoid feelings of stigmatization, shame, and failure. Sometimes patients will benefit from a program specially designed for them but will appreciate if it is located in a community setting (e.g., a community college rather than a psychiatry outpatient department). I believe there is also a place, however, for social clubs set up only for psychiatric patients.

Example

_____ House was a social club designed for psychiatric patients and located in a beautiful restored house in a central area of the city. Patients appreciated being able to attend when they wished, and to play games, prepare meals, and socialize with peers. I was a consultant to the House and met with the staff once per month. In one meeting, a staff member complained: "Our clients really enjoy coming here, but perhaps they are getting too dependent. How can we get them to leave us and enter the community?" I explained that for these clients, this House was their community. We talked about staff frustration at not being able to cure these patients. Many staff members had a model of all mental illness as temporary and saw the House as a transition between hospital and full functioning. We discussed chronic mental illness and the development of realistic hopes and expectations for the clients.

Vocational and Educational Programs

Vocational and educational programs are important components in rehabilitation of the schizophrenic patient. Having the status of worker or student improves self-esteem and often provides a positive identity to a demoralized psychiatric patient. Work also offers the patient an income, a constructive daily activity, and an opportunity for social interactions (Wasylenki et al. 1986). As with recreational activities, a range of options is necessary. For some patients, a return to competitive employment is feasible, perhaps after vocational assessment and preparation. These individuals may continue to need vocational support, for example, a weekly meeting with peers and a vocational supervisor. Often patients find the interpersonal stresses of work more challenging than the actual job performance. Many schizophrenic patients cannot perform adequately in a competitive job but may be satisfied with a sheltered workshop. For some patients, attending a community college or university is a very gratifying experience.

Example
Ralph is a 52-year-old schizophrenic single man. He has been able to hold a job as a civil servant doing simple clerical tasks in spite of periodic relapses. However, he is teased by his co-workers who ridicule his formal, pedantic manner. Consequently he gets little satisfaction from work. Recently he has started to take evening courses at university, one course per year toward a B.A. degree. He is extremely proud of his accomplishments so far and looks forward to getting his degree in the year 2005.

The physician is not likely to know of all the vocational and educational opportunities and therefore needs to be able to refer a patient to a suitable counselor and maintain contact with this person. Unfortunately, mainstream vocational agencies (government and private) often quickly dismiss a psychiatric patient as unsuitable, and specialized vocational services frequently plug the patient into available slots that may be too simple and demeaning. The physician who has a good understanding and respect for a patient can help him or her obtain the optimal services.

Example
Ann is a 42-year-old schizophrenic woman. She has a B.A. in sociology and left the university when she was unable to complete her master's thesis. Since then her job performance has steadily deteriorated, so that in the past 2 years she has had many clerical positions, which she either quits or is fired from. After several weeks in any job she feels that her peers are jealous of her and are ridiculing her. She was unwilling to accept a referral to a vocational service for psychiatric patients. Previous experiences with such agencies had felt humiliating because she had been urged to attend a sheltered workshop. Unfortunately, employment agencies no longer welcomed her because of her poor record. I referred her to a vocational service where she underwent extensive psychological and vocational testing, only to be told at the end that she was incapable of working. However, she remained committed to finding a good job. She now

accepted a referral to a psychiatric vocational service. In my referral, I emphasized her skills and ambition and her previous negative experiences. This time she was offered a comprehensive evaluation, and it was found that she could carry out research activities in a library very effectively if she did not have to meet deadlines or compete with other employees.

Financial Services

Schizophrenic patients generally have to subsist on an inadequate income. The psychiatrist can at least ensure that the patient receives all the financial aid that he or she is entitled to. Holcomb and Ahr (1988) found in a sample of young adult chronic patients only 15.4% were receiving Supplemental Security Income (SSI) or Social Security Disability Insurance (SSDI) even though they were severely impaired and generally unemployed. Psychiatrists need to be familiar with the criteria for eligibility for government assistance (Okpaku 1988). These criteria may subtly change over time as they are often reinterpreted by zealous bureaucrats. The psychiatrist needs to find out by talking to disability workers and to other psychiatrists not only the written rules and standards, but also the informal working practice.

Example
I was finding that several patients whom I had considered eligible for disability pension were denied this pension. I discovered that I used to answer on the physician's report that I considered a patient unable to return to work for an indeterminate period and this was an acceptable response, but now applications were refused unless the answer specified that the patient would remain disabled for over 1 year.

Example
In the previous example with Kent, I decided that I would intervene with the more flexible, rational party, my patient rather than the disability system. I advised my patient to pay his parents an increased room and board allowance rather than spend

his money extravagantly. His parents could then save money for him for his future needs, and his bank balance would not surpass the allowed limit.

Additional Services

The schizophrenic patient may benefit from many additional services and relationships. Social skills training can teach the patient to respond more effectively in social situations and express feelings in a more appropriate manner (Chapter 8). The model for skills training consists of role playing by the patient and modeling, prompting, feedback, and reinforcement by the therapist (Liberman et al. 1986). The therapist needs to try to promote generalization of skills from the office to the community by teaching the patient's network (family, friends, other workers) to reinforce the patient's developing skills, and preparing the patient for a wide variety of new situations.

Life skills training is often invaluable in preparing a patient to live independently, where he or she is required to budget money, shop, prepare meals, and do housekeeping. Wong et al. (1988) demonstrated that chronic schizophrenic patients could be taught to improve their personal grooming skills in a 5-week training program, and the results were fully maintained 6 months later. Improved social competence in areas such as grooming and appearance predicts a more successful adaptation to community living (Wong et al. 1988). These programs are sometimes offered at community centers and sometimes only by psychiatric agencies. The psychiatrist must know the patient well to assess which program is suitable.

Example
Larry is a young schizophrenic man who insisted on obtaining a high-functioning job immediately and putting his illness behind him. However, his attempts to return to work had been unsuccessful. I recommended that he attend a program where the emphasis was on classroom instruction of social, vocational, and life skills, followed by placement in a supervised job. He in-

sisted on bypassing phase one and entering the job situation right away. I spoke to the program coordinator and pointed out that Larry had serious deficiencies in life skills that I hoped could be remedied in phase one of their program. In this instance, I believed the program coordinator was being too flexible in his willingness to accept Larry into the employment phase. After several conversations with me and his family, Larry agreed to participate in the full program, and achieved good results.

Social network therapy is a relatively new method of therapy that attempts to normalize a patient's network (Morin and Seedman 1986). A schizophrenic patient often has a very limited network of people connected to him or her. These relationships may consist almost exclusively of family ties, and because the family feels burdened these ties may be negative. The patient may lack reciprocal relationships, and may always find himself or herself in the same stereotypical patient role. The network therapist attempts to link patients to new people and programs and help them broaden their identity. The therapist may hold meetings with the entire network to plan changes. This unique service is best offered by therapists with special training in it. However, the physician can often have useful meetings with the patient and significant others in the patient's life.

Example

Sally is a 21-year-old single schizophrenic woman. Although she has experienced psychotic symptoms for 5 years, she has only recently accepted treatment. She was responding well but then started to resist again. I discovered that a cousin from France had been visiting the family and was espousing his theories of mental illness to her, specifically, that it does not exist, and only natural methods of healing should be used. We had a meeting with her and her cousin (as well as her father and sister). When she told her cousin more about her psychotic symptoms and I offered scientific information about schizophrenia, his opposition to her treatment faded and he became an ally rather than an opponent of appropriate therapy.

Difficulties and Dangers in Networking

The psychiatrist primarily involved with the schizophrenic patient needs to develop an understanding and rapport not only with the patient but also with the patient's other helpers. Does this dual role present any difficulties? I believe it does, and these problems need to be addressed.

The first issue is confidentiality. How can the psychiatrist speak to many other individuals and agencies, family, other professionals, and governmental and insurance agents without betraying the patient's private confidences? Patients should be informed at the outset of therapy that it is often desirable for the doctor to speak to and meet with other professionals in order to offer the patient coordinated treatment. The doctor is often asked to provide information to agencies and other service providers. The patient is reassured that only necessary information will be shared and only with the patient's explicit permission. When the psychiatrist wishes to meet with others in the patient's network, the patient will generally be invited. If the patient refuses to allow such sharing of information, his or her wishes prevail but he or she is informed that the treatment may consequently suffer.

A second issue is the danger of overinvolvement and paternalism. The psychiatrist and other professionals may make too many decisions "in the best interest of the patient" without sufficiently involving the patient. It must be remembered that an indispensable principle in the rehabilitation of a psychiatric patient is to include him or her as a partner in the selection of goals and the decisions and plans directed toward the implementation of those goals (Anthony and Liberman 1986). With some patients, the psychiatrist may need to monitor the delivery of services and provide liaison to agencies indefinitely. With others, the doctor's role may be phased out as the patient becomes more autonomous.

Payment for indirect services is another difficulty. Government and insurance providers often pay for only direct clinical activities and not for equally necessary networking activities. Such a policy constitutes a subtle form of discrimination against chronic patients who require such services and against practitioners who are willing and interested in working with these patients. When such payment is lacking, networking activities can be conducted in the presence of the patient whenever possible and billed for as family therapy. As discussed above, the participation of the patient is desirable for clinical and ethical reasons. The psychiatrist needs to learn to become resourceful and efficient in providing networking services. A nurse practitioner or sometimes a receptionist/secretary can often help with these valuable services. The patient may develop an additional comfortable relationship with a friendly, informal but respectful receptionist. Coordination can often be achieved by a brief letter or telephone call.

Conclusion

The aim of networking activity is to improve the quality of the patient's life by facilitating the ability of agencies to provide appropriate and truly useful services to the patient. A patient's feelings of shame and demoralization and self-stigmatization can best be lessened in therapy when we are also working simultaneously to decrease the stigmatization of psychiatric patients by society. Society includes the patient's network of family and friends, private and public agencies, and ourselves. We must always advocate for a tolerant and fair attitude toward the mentally ill.

The schizophrenic patient suffers from internal splits and fragmentation. He often lacks a cohesive sense of who he is, what he can do, what he can aspire to. How ironical that such individuals often have to encounter an equally fragmented and contradictory external world. By coordinating the services and eliminating the inconsistencies between the helpers, the patient is offered a view of a more rational and more inviting world and is aided in his or her journey of self-healing.

References

Anthony WA, Liberman RP: The practice of psychiatric rehabilitation: historical, conceptual, and research base. Schizophr Bull 12:543–559, 1986

Farmer S: Medical problems of chronic patients in a community support program. Hosp Community Psychiatry 38:745–749, 1987

Holcomb WR, Ahr PR: Disability and welfare benefits for young adult chronic patients. Hosp Community Psychiatry 39:1104–1106, 1988

Intagliata J: Improving the quality of community care for the chronically mentally disabled: the role of case management. Schizophr Bull 8:655–674, 1982

Lamb HR: Treating the Long-Term Mentally Ill. San Francisco, CA, Jossey-Bass, 1982

Liberman RP, Mueser KT, Wallace CJ, et al: Training skills in the psychiatrically disabled: learning coping and competence. Schizophr Bull 12:631–646, 1986

Meyerson AT, Herman GS: What's new in aftercare? A review of recent literature. Hosp Community Psychiatry 34:333–342, 1983

Morin RC, Seedman E: A social network approach and the revolving door patient. Schizophr Bull 12:262–273, 1986

Okpaku SO: The psychiatrist and the social security disability insurance and supplemental security income programs. Hosp Community Psychiatry 39:879–883, 1988

Talbott JA: The Chronic Mental Patient, Five Years Later. Orlando, FL, Grune and Stratton, 1984

Wasylenki D, Glaser F, Goering P, et al: Discussion Paper: Components of Care for Schizophrenic Patients. Advisory Group on the Coordination of Metropolitan Toronto Mental Health Services, 1986

Wong SE, Flanagan SG, Kuehnel TG, et al: Training chronic mental patients to independently practice personal grooming skills. Hosp Community Psychiatry 39:874–879, 1988

Chapter 10

Dealing With Crisis

RODNEY O. N. SLONIM, M.D., F.R.C.P.(C)

Chapter 10

Dealing With Crisis

Crisis is defined as a response to external or internal stress that cannot be managed by the usual coping mechanisms of the person stressed. It is experienced when the ego cannot solve acute problems and represents in the schizophrenic patient not only a disequilibrium in an already "fragile" ego state but, more commonly, a disorganization of already compromised ego functioning (Langsley 1981). Although Caplan (1964) viewed crisis as an opportunity for mastery, he also recognized that in the attempt at achieving a solution to the crisis state (intolerable when prolonged), the individual may develop a new state of equilibrium that is maladaptive. In a patient who is already schizophrenic or whose crisis may be the initial sign of a schizophrenic illness, that is, the "Trema" (Conrad 1958), this is characterized by decompensation and marked regression.

It is important to remember that the crisis is a response to a stress and represents both the type of stress and the patient's special susceptibility to the stress. In the patient with schizophrenia, as Baldwin (1978) states, the crisis already reflects existing psychopathology with lowered vulnerability, which necessitates long-term treatment, already perhaps in effect prior to the crisis intervention. Since crisis does not occur in isolation, the social and family system must be carefully considered.

I will elaborate on the following questions: What are the types of crises commonly seen in the office treatment of schizophrenia? What kinds of interventions are indicated?

179

What are the interventions required? And what are the legal implications in terms of the crisis?

The types of crises can be divided, first, by what I will define as *acute* and *chronic*.

Acute Crises

By acute crises, I mean those states in a schizophrenic patient that can be diagnosed as an acute psychosis or crisis state related to the toxic consequences of medication.

Acute Psychosis

This is a rapidly developing pathological state characterized by disorganized thinking, distorted perceptions, intense and unrealistic feelings, and inappropriate behavior. The patient demonstrates gross impairment of his or her reality perception and ability to distinguish his or her inner experience from the outside. The patient therefore cannot relate or communicate to others normally or meet the ordinary demands of life. Characteristically, the patient presents with illogical, disconnected thinking, delusions, and hallucinations, usually of the auditory type. In this state, which may vary from less to more disorganized, the patient who arrives at or, most commonly, is brought to your office by a family member, friend, or health care professional may present with inability to maintain himself or herself, may be at risk for suicide, or may be potentially homicidal or violent.

The key in treating acutely psychotic schizophrenic patients in your office is based upon rapid evaluation. Gerson and Bassuk's (1980) system, I feel, is particularly useful. They recommend evaluation of 1) the nature and availability of a support system and the patient's capacity to use it, 2) the degree of dangerousness to self or others, 3) past psychiatric history and present psychiatric symptoms, 4) ability to care for self, 5) motivation and capacity to participate in treatment, 6) the request of family and/or the patient for a specific type of help, and 7) the medical status of the patient. These factors influence your decision to initiate treatment immediately, that is, crisis intervention, prompt psychopharmacologic intervention, and facilitation of disposition elsewhere, that is, home or hospital, or, in many cases, to initiate all of the above.

Potential for violence. The assessment of violence potential is particularly important, since there may be a strong association between violent behavior and acute schizophrenic disturbance (Rofman et al. 1980; Skodol and Karasu 1978). Violent behavior is more commonly seen in younger, male schizophrenic patients and is associated with the presence of acute paranoid symptoms (Tardiff and Sweillam 1980). A careful assessment of violent or homicidal behavior is mandatory. The presence of paranoid symptoms is of particular concern, because the patient may strike back at people who they believe wish them "ill." When a delusional system exists that implicates one specific "villain" within an acute psychotic state, this is truly an extremely dangerous situation and inevitably requires hospitalization. Command hallucinations ordering the patient to commit violence also is a very high-risk symptom for violent potential. This equally requires hospitalization. The presence of intoxication with alcohol or drugs such as amphetamines or phencyclidine also compounds the danger.

The approach to a belligerent and potentially violent schizophrenic patient is understandably a calm, reasonable, and cautious one. In the setting of one's office, the prime concern must be for the safety of oneself, the patient, staff if present, and the caretakers who have brought the patient for assessment. Needless to say, an assessment frequently can be conducted over the telephone with the concerned significant other prior to the patient's arrival at your office, and where one is concerned about violence potential an appropriate referral to an emergency service in a general hospital or psychiatric facility may be the first choice. Contact with police in extremely serious circumstances may also be necessary, taking into account the issues of confidentiality but respecting the need for protection of life (Appelbaum 1981; Schmid et al. 1983).

In the assessment of an acutely psychotic patient with some signs of possible violent behavior in your office, a calm, confident, cautious approach is required, with awareness of your own fears and anxiety and the recognition that these feelings mirror similar feelings in the patient and reflect his or her own fear of the threat of violence and frustration in trying to avoid it. You should acknowledge the danger but not allow fear to dominate (Dibella 1979; Lion and Pasternak 1973). Attempting to establish rapport by appealing to the patient's strengths, structuring his or her expectation, encouraging impulse control, and explaining alternative treatment choices is critical.

From your first intervention with the patient, you should underline empathically that the top priority for you and the patient is for the patient to maintain control, which is a prerequisite to effective treatment. If the patient is unable to cooperate, then rather than bargaining or arguing with the patient, effective alternative treatment, involving the caretakers, must be initiated. Throughout the assessment, constant explanation should be given to the patient in a calm and straightforward manner. For example, the prescription of medication may be necessary or, if the patient refuses the medication, then an appropriate alternative is to direct the caretakers to accompany the patient to the nearest treatment facility. It has been my experience that when one addresses and acknowledges the inner fear of patients, they will agree to the use of medication. Haloperidol intramuscularly in doses of 5 mg to begin with is recommended as an effective drug. This will help the patient by allaying his or her anxiety and reducing the inner tension and terror of the possibility of losing control. Rapid neuroleptization should be reserved for a hospital setting with adequate support and monitoring facilities. The importance of respecting the optimal distance with a paranoid patient must be emphasized since any intrusion into his or her fragile boundary can be interpreted as a threat and lead to an aggressive response.

This clinical example will illustrate some of these issues.

Example
A 35-year-old married paranoid schizophrenic man has delusions of infidelity involving his wife. These delusions have escalated to the point where he has had violent verbal outbursts directed toward his wife, who now is terrified of him. Along with this escalation, he has become increasingly more erratic in his relationship with his 8-year-old son, whose paternity he doubts, punishing him for spilling his food at the dinner table by forcefully flicking his forehead to the point of inducing crying. Accompanied by his wife, the patient arrives at the psychiatrist's office demonstrating a vigilant and suspicious affect. He feels justified in his attitudes and behavior. He is distrustful of the psychiatrist and relates that he is very distrustful of his bosses at work. He has recently taken a leave of absence from work. He confides that he has a plan to stab his wife to death when he finally proves her infidelity beyond any doubt to himself. Given the grave nature of his presentation, he is encouraged to enter a hospital and agrees, somewhat reluctantly. He voluntarily enters a psychiatric inpatient unit and is immediately placed on close observation, and a course of haloperidol is initiated.

Potential for suicidal behavior. In the case of acute psychosis in a schizophrenic patient with suicidal potential, again a careful assessment with particular attention paid to the suicidal evaluation must be done. Since self-destructive urges may be unchecked by internal controls and acted upon, and delusional patients may suddenly act on impulses that lead to their death although unintended, psychotic schizophrenic patients with suicidal intent present a very high risk. This is particularly so if command hallucinations are present that demand that they kill themselves. Bright, young, psychologically aware patients who are decompensating for the first time may present also as very high suicidal risks because of their fear of long-term deterioration. Again, urgent hospitalization is indicated in all of the above cases. In my own clinical experience, just as the recognition of fear, frustration, and perceived threat in oneself is helpful in identifying the threat of violence in the patient, so too is the recognition of the feeling of hopeless or confused despair in oneself a valuable tool in evaluating suicidal risk in a psychotic schizophrenic patient. This clinical example serves to poignantly illustrate this fact.

Example
A 27-year-old graduate student in electrical engineering presents with disorganized thinking, ideas of reference, extreme agitation, restlessness, and auditory hallucinations that consist of his professor's voice telling him to jump in front of a subway train. He knows that he must obey "the voice." This is the young man's first psychotic break. He has a family member, a cousin, whom he describes as brilliant with all his life ahead of him, presently living in a supervised home for chronic schizophrenic patients and "doing nothing," as he states, "but watching TV and smoking." This patient is assessed in your office and is hospitalized following the first assessment. However, his hospital course is marked by slow deterioration, which continues following discharge. In spite of careful monitoring and awareness of his high risk, he successfully commits suicide 1 year to the day of his first hospitalization, a tragedy for all involved, in spite of heightened clinical awareness, and sensitivity to his predicament. He had successfully concealed both his planning for the act and the act itself. Postmortem psychiatric review with all the staff involved in his treatment fails to turn up any single clue that could have led to the prevention of this suicide. Even the awareness of the anniversary date of his first hospitalization, which was raised with him, was not responded to in any way that was suggestive of any planned act.

This, of course, is an extreme example, but nevertheless highlights the problem in these patients with suicidal potential. More often than not, the risk of suicide diminishes with active treatment and with the addition of antidepressant medication prescribed on an individual basis according to the clinical picture of the patient.

Crisis States Related to the Toxic Consequences of Medication

Acute dystonia. This term refers to the abnormal involuntary movements of various types and oculogyric crises that typically occur in the immediate period following the administration of antipsychotic medication or following a significant increase in the dosage prescribed. Usually this reaction is manifested by involuntary muscle contractions involving the face, mouth, tongue, neck, and jaw. Trismus, that is, "lockjaw," and opisthotonos (spasms of the neck that arch the head backward and eye closures as distinct from the fixed gaze found in oculogyric crises) are other forms of clinical presentation.

Young, male schizophrenic patients on high potency antipsychotic medication develop acute dystonias more frequently. Although these reactions are particularly distressing to patients and their families, they are easily diagnosed and treated. These reactions are rarely dangerous except in rare instances where respiratory distress, with its fatal potential, has developed. Treatment is generally dramatically successful. After a comprehensive history and mental status examination to rule out the rare possibility of hypocalcemia, administration parenterally of a benzodiazepine such as diazepam (Valium) should be initiated. If administered intravenously, then up to 10 mg should be given slowly at a rate of 5 mg per minute. Although diazepam is safe and does not add additional anticholinergic effects, emergency equipment to maintain the airway should be available in your office, since diazepam is a central nervous system depressant (Gelenberg 1983).

Fifteen milligrams of the antihistamine diphenhydramine (Benadryl) can also be administered and is very effective. One milligram of anticholinergic, antiparkinsonian drugs such as benztropine (Cogentin) is also commonly used. One of the above drugs may be prescribed to the patient following the immediate relief of the acute dystonia, in order to maintain the relief of the dystonia. The lowest possible dose should be used.

If successful resolution is maintained, the dose can usually be subsequently tapered and the medication ultimately discontinued. This begs the question of whether placing schizophrenic patients in the high-risk category (that is, young, male, on high potency medications) on concomitant antiparkinsonian therapy is indicated (Smith 1980). In my experience, initiating treatment with a low potency antipsychotic drug is preferable if clinically indicated; if not, then for those patients for whom acute dystonia may interfere with the therapeutic relationship, I would add an appropriate counteractive agent as a prophylactic.

Example

A 23-year-old man recently discharged from a general hospital inpatient unit for his first schizophrenic break is brought to my office by his parents. He presents with a locked jaw, fixed gaze, and arching of his neck. His haloperidol has recently been increased by 10 mg per day. He is frightened, and his parents are extremely concerned and anxious but have been obviously carefully prepared by the hospital staff for this occurrence. The patient responds, after careful assessment of his clinical presentation and collateral history from parents and hospital, to a 5-mg dose intramuscularly of diazepam. A further 5 mg of diazepam is given orally following his relief, and a week's supply of diazepam 5 mg twice daily, along with a reduction of his haloperidol by 10 mg, is prescribed. The recent increase was apparently warranted on the basis of a presumed increase in his psychotic symptoms, specifically, ideas of reference. However, it became readily apparent that his parents were frightened and overprotective now that the patient had returned home. Along with this, the patient was responding to their increased anxiety and was manifesting increased concerns about his well-being as well. My recommendation to the parents and this young man was that the parents join Friends of Schizophrenics, a local support group for families and friends of schizophrenic patients, and that this young man be enrolled in a community outreach program. This alleviated both the parents' and this young man's anxiety. A frank discussion about the meaning of schizophrenia followed and helped to dispel their unrealistic yet poignant fears.

Often this empathic psychotherapeutic approach can mitigate the overreliance on medication in dealing with the common emergence of posthospital separation and reentry anxiety.

Akathisia. Akathisia is a subjective symptom described by the patient as a compulsion to be in motion. The patient describes an inner restlessness, a need to move for the sake of moving. Patients with akathisia can be observed to be pacing, to be markedly restless, and to fidget. Although akathisia can occur early on in the course of antipsychotic drug treatment, it may also not occur until much later. Again, the incidence of akathisia is increased with the use of high potency medication. Both the natural course and the response to treatment in akathisic patients is uncertain. However, it represents a particularly distressing symptom to patients that can seriously interfere with their compliance to treatment. It must be distinguished from anxiety or, in rare cases, a somatic hallucination. Treatment options consist of reducing the dose of the antipsychotic medication, substituting a lower potency agent, or adding an anticholinergic, antiparkinsonian drug, an antihistamine, or benzodiazepine. These drugs should be prescribed as oral medication, but the results may be much less successful than in the treatment of acute dystonias.

Example
Jim is a 26-year-old young man with a diagnosis of paranoid schizophrenia. This diagnosis was made 7 months prior to his office consultation with me. He is presently on haloperidol 20 mg twice daily, which he takes orally. He presents in my office complaining of not being able to keep still, as if his "insides are moving," and paces incessantly in the office. He is clearly in acute distress, stating that he feels like killing himself to relieve these intense feelings, although he has no fixed plan and does not want to die. He has been unable to work since these symptoms became intense the previous day. After a careful and complete psychiatric assessment, akathisia is diagnosed. His haloperidol is reduced to 20 mg, that is, 10 mg twice daily, and

diazepam 5 mg twice daily is added. Over the course of the next 3 days, his symptoms improve sufficiently to allow him to return to work. The restless inner feeling he has described has diminished to a very significant degree. There is no evidence of suicidal ideation, which clearly was related to his intense discomfort.

Parkinson's syndrome. Tremor, commonly "a pill-rolling movement" with the thumb rubbing against the pad of the index finger; rigidity—the patient must feel rigid with an increased resistance to passive motion and a slow return from a raised position—with tremor coexisting, the rigidity has the feel of a "cogwheel"; and akinesia or bradykinesia, that is, the reduction in movement in the absence of paralysis, comprise the classic triad of signs in Parkinson's syndrome. In neuroleptic-induced Parkinson's syndrome, the tremor is characteristically bilateral, rigidity occurs more frequently than tremor, but akinesia is the most frequently occurring sign (Rifkin et al. 1975). In the severe forms of the syndrome, rigidity may appear or become the waxy flexibility with sustained postures characteristic of catatonia, or bradykinesia may develop into catatonic immobility.

Often in less severe forms of the Parkinson's syndrome, a diagnosis of depression may be considered when in fact the apathy, boredom, or a "zombie-like" appearance are manifestations of the Parkinson's syndrome itself. The onset is usually within a period of weeks to months following the initiation of antipsychotic drug therapy. It occurs more frequently in women and the elderly. High potency drugs have a higher incidence of this side effect. The development of tolerance is common. But the disorder may persist and require treatment. Other signs associated with this syndrome are seborrhea and drooling. A late occurring sign is the "rabbit" syndrome characterized by a rapid tremor of the mouth and jaw.

Treatment can be divided into two categories. The first depends on decreasing the dose of the antipsychotic medication or substituting a low potency antipsychotic agent. Both operate

188

by decreasing the degree of dopamine blockade at the synaptic receptor. The second is the utilization of an antiparkinsonian agent. In your office, the choice is often between a drug such as amantadine or alternative antiparkinsonian drugs. Amantadine is a dopamine agonist that has few anticholinergic effects and therefore is useful in the treatment of patients who are sensitive to anticholinergic reactions; doses employed orally are usually in the range of 100 mg twice daily to three times daily. The alternative antiparkinsonian drugs have anticholinergic and/or antihistamine properties. Benztropine (Cogentin), for example, can be given in doses of 1 mg to 6 mg per day orally but may be given parenterally to initiate treatment.

Just a brief mention of the anticholinergic syndrome—which can be seen in patients on antipsychotic medication and particularly those patients who have been prescribed antiparkinsonian agents as well, or are also taking tricyclic antidepressants such as imipramine or have added antihistamines, hypnotic agents, or many over-the-counter preparations (Smith 1980). Acute overdoses may cause anticholinergic crisis and may present in your office with the classic symptoms of dry mouth, red face, dilated pupils, increased heart rate, elevated temperature, and rapid pulse with widened pulse pressure. The elderly and children are particularly sensitive to this side effect.

Treatment with physostigmine salicylate 1–2 mg intramuscularly in the office will bring dramatic relief of symptoms. Physostigmine should be infused slowly if given intravenously —1 mg over 2 minutes—and the cardiac status should be monitored carefully with respiratory support available. I prefer for this reason the intramuscular route in the office setting. If no improvement occurs in 15–20 minutes, another similar dose should be given. Up to 4 mg may be given over 15 minutes. Since the toxic agent may be eliminated or degraded more slowly than physostigmine, additional doses of 1–2 mg at 30-minute intervals may be necessary even with successful initial treatment. The use of physostigmine should be avoided in the presence of unstable vital signs (Granacher and Baldessarini

1975). In that case, your patient should be monitored in a hospital setting with consultation.

Chronic Crises

By chronic crises, I refer to the crises of everyday life as experienced frequently by schizophrenic patients. The "caretaking crisis," as described by Langsley (Langsley et al. 1968), where the caretaker or network of caretakers, that is, family members, agency workers, landlord, or employer, withdraws support from the patient, even for reasons unrelated to his or her caretaking role, may lead to a crisis. In this instance, only careful inquiry and "attuned" understanding of the patient's social network and its critical importance will delineate the causative factors for the patient's apparent crisis.

Frequently, for many schizophrenic patients, no antecedent stress is apparent or, if present, may be felt to be insignificant in importance to the observer yet exquisitely painful to the patient. This clinical example is illustrative.

Example
A 45-year-old woman with a 15-year history of chronic schizophrenia is standing at a corner waiting for the stoplight to change from red to green in order to cross the street. At the moment of that change, she begins to cry and is filled with visions of her deceased mother, whose death occurred 6 weeks prior to this time and for whom she was unable to mourn. She presents in my office agitated, depressed, but with no increase in her psychotic symptoms. The psychological trigger for her was the change of the red light, meaning death for her, to green, meaning life, which allowed the emergence of the mourning process. Although frightened, she also stated that she felt great relief.

Schwartz and Myers (1977a) found that in schizophrenia the vulnerability is so diffuse and extreme that virtually any environmental change can precipitate decompensation or acute psychosis. However, they have also shown that among schizophrenic patients psychosocial stresses may be associated with elevation of anxiety, depression, and somatic concerns, rather than acute psychoses (Schwartz and Myers 1977b).

Legal Implications in the Office Treatment of Schizophrenia

The legal implications and issues to be considered in the office treatment of schizophrenia are complex. The laws in regard to the rights of the mentally ill patient vary from state to state in the United States, and from province to province in Canada. It is imperative that each psychiatrist be fully versed in the local laws that are applicable to medical practice in general and to a psychiatric practice, that is, mental health legislation in particular.

Issues such as informed consent, assessment of competence to decide on treatment issues, substitutive consent, criteria for involuntary hospitalization, treatment refusal by competent involuntary patients, treatment of incompetent involuntary patients, access to medical records, legal rights, confidentiality, dangerousness, suicidality, legal liability, and standards of care must be carefully studied and thoroughly understood (Hoffman 1987).

In the clinical example of the 35-year-old male paranoid schizophrenic patient, several legal issues were raised. The first was the potential dangerousness of this patient, particularly to his wife and son. Second, the possibility of involuntary hospitalization was anticipated although this in the end, fortunately, did not become an issue. Third, the issue of confidentiality was raised in relation to the patient's statement in confidence to the clinician that he had in fact thought of killing his wife by stabbing her, along with an unrelenting conviction that he would soon have evidence of her infidelity. What if this patient had refused treatment? What were the responsibilities of the clinician to the patient's wife and child? The landmark *Tarasoff* case comes to mind (*Tarasoff v. Regents of the University of California,* 1976). "When a therapist determines, or pur-

191

suant to the standards of his profession should determine, that his patient presents a serious danger of violence to another, he incurs an obligation to use reasonable care to protect the intended victim against such danger." Appelbaum has written on the *Tarasoff* decision and I recommend his article regarding this complicated area involved in the duty to warn (Appelbaum 1981). Why did this patient agree to voluntary hospitalization, while in many other similar situations, there is often outright refusal? (Appelbaum and Hamm 1982). What if this patient, upon admission to hospital, refused treatment? (Appelbaum 1983). These are dilemmas we face daily, and they can only be competently dealt with by a careful psychiatric history and mental status examination along with a substantive grasp of the mental health legislation in your own practice area.

Occasionally there are cases that present as serious risks where no intervention can be applied because the patient or the patient's representative refuses treatment and is legally and psychiatrically competent to make that decision.

Summary

In summary, dealing with crisis in the office treatment of schizophrenia has focused on the definition of crisis. Its "acute" and "chronic" aspects were presented with a focus on the management of acute psychotic episodes, toxic drug reactions, violent potential, and suicidality. The legal implications and their importance in treatment were highlighted.

References

Appelbaum PS: *Tarasoff:* an update on the duty to warn. Hosp Community Psychiatry 32:14–15, 1981

Appelbaum PS: Refusing treatment: the uncertainty continues. Hosp Community Psychiatry 34:11–12, 1983

Appelbaum PS, Hamm RM: Decision to seek commitment:

psychiatric decision making in a legal context. Arch Gen Psychiatry 39:447–451, 1982

Baldwin BA: A paradigm for the classification of emotional crisis: implication for crisis intervention. Am J Orthopsychiatry 48:538–551, 1978

Caplan G: Principles of Preventive Psychiatry. New York, Basic Books, 1964

Conrad K: Die beginnende Schizophrenie. Versuch einer Gestaltanalyse des Wahns (Commencing Schizophrenia: An Attempt at a Gestalt Analysis of Delusion). Stuttgart, Thieme, 1958

Dibella CA: Educating staff to manage threatening paranoid patients. Am J Psychiatry 136:333–335, 1979

Gelenberg AJ: Acute psychoses, in The Practitioner's Guide to Psychoactive Drugs, 2nd Edition. Edited by Bassuk EL, Schoonover SC, Gelenberg AJ. New York, Plenum Publishing, 1983, pp 64–79

Gerson S, Bassuk E: Psychiatric emergencies: an overview. Am J Psychiatry 137:1–11, 1980

Granacher RD, Baldessarini RJ: Physostigmine: its use in acute anticholinergic syndrome with antidepressant and antiparkinson drugs. Arch Gen Psychiatry 32:375–379, 1975

Hoffman BF: The Mental Health Act: civil rights, patient treatment, and the psychiatrist. Ontario Medical Review 54:10–18, 1987

Langsley DG: Crisis intervention: an update. Curr Psychiatr Ther 20:19–37, 1981

Langsley DG, Pittman FS, Machotka P, et al: Family crisis therapy results and implications. Fam Process 7:145–158, 1968

Lion JR, Pasternak SA: Countertransference reactions to violent patients. Am J Psychiatry 130:207–210, 1973

Rifkin A, Quitkin F, Klein DF: Akinesia: a poorly recognized drug-induced extrapyramidal behavior disorder. Arch Gen Psychiatry 32:642–674, 1975

Rofman ES, Askinazi C, Fant E: The prediction of dangerous behavior in emergency civil commitment. Am J Psychiatry 137:1061–1064, 1980

Schmid D, Appelbaum PS, Roth LH, et al: Confidentiality in psychiatry: a study of the patient's view. Hosp Community Psychiatry 34:353–355, 1983

Schwartz CC, Myers JK: Life events and schizophrenia, I: comparison of schizophrenics with a community sample. Arch Gen Psychiatry 34:1238–1241, 1977a

Schwartz CC, Myers JK: Life events and schizophrenia, II: impact of life events on symptom configuration. Arch Gen Psychiatry 34:1242–1245, 1977b

Skodol AE, Karasu TB: Emergency psychiatry and the assaultive patient. Am J Psychiatry 135:202–205, 1978

Smith JM: Abuse of the antiparkinson drugs: a review of the literature. J Clin Psychiatry 41:351–354, 1980

Tarasoff v. Regents of the University of California, 551 P 2d 334 (Cal 1976)

Tardiff K, Sweillam A: Assault, suicide and mental illness. Arch Gen Psychiatry 37:164–169, 1980

Chapter 11

Conclusion: Essentials and Prospects for the Future

STANLEY E. GREBEN, M.D., F.R.C.P.(C)

Chapter 11

Conclusion: Essentials and Prospects for the Future

*I*t has been our intention in this book to address the needs of those many patients who are afflicted with the disorder that we call *schizophrenia*. In order to do that in a clear manner, we have divided our presentation into various parts, each of which has its own importance. The purpose of this chapter is to bring some overview and some synthesis to our subject. This includes the task of highlighting what is essential in the office treatment of schizophrenia, as well as some ideas of what the future might hold.

When one looks at the history of the treatment of this major psychiatric disorder, it is clear that there has been oscillation between two quite different positions. One position is that persons so afflicted cannot be fundamentally changed through treatment and that as a result they are best removed from normal society for the protection of both themselves and the other members of society. It was as a result of this attitude that large mental hospitals were built in the last century, giving expression to the attitude: "Out of mind, out of sight." The opposite position is that incarceration in large mental hospitals not only doesn't help such patients, but in fact further hurts them, adding the ignominy of neglect or abuse and the stigmata of isolation and understimulation to the signs and symptoms that are indigenous to the disorder itself. The community mental health movement has taken such a position and was supported by those who felt very keenly the need to protect all citizens, even those who are ill, from infringements upon their basic civil rights.

The position we have taken is at neither of these two extremes, but is rather as follows. Schizophrenia is a chronic disorder, ordinarily. It arises out of, in many instances, damaged areas in the brain, and in many cases there is an inherited genetic vulnerability that leads to this damage. Our tools for demonstrating such central nervous system deficits have become much more powerful in recent decades, but they are still relatively weak for the diagnostic task at hand. Added to whatever central nervous system pathology is present in such patients are difficulties that arise out of the psychosocial effects of that pathology. The patient is different and so the treatment that he or she receives at the hands of family and friends is different. As a consequence, to morphological pathology is added psychological pathology, and the afflicted person is even less likely to be able to pursue a normal life. At the same time, not only the life of the patient is affected, but so are the lives of those who are close to the patient. Difficult psychological habits are built up in the patient, the family and, perhaps, friends and colleagues. In the field of psychiatry in this century, a great deal has been learned about schizophrenia and about the people who suffer with the disorder. As is always the way with science, knowledge is gained piecemeal, some here and some there, and the various approaches to the patient and the illness have been developed individually and separately. Achieving synthesis in any field is at least as demanding as was discovering the various pieces of truth in the first instance, and this is the case as well in this field.

Many schizophrenic patients have been helped in psychiatric hospitals and, increasingly, in departments of psychiatry in general hospitals. Too often, unfortunately, the inpatient treatment has been seen as all that could be done, so that an improved patient is discharged to an environment that is inadequately supportive. He or she is not offered follow-up treatment that would, if made available, allow him or her to make further gains and to consolidate those gains. As a consequence, we take the position that as important as inpatient treatment of schizophrenia can be, even more important in the long run is office treatment. Hospital treatment has natural limits, because of its great expense and, in addition, as mentioned above, because it adds its own signs and symptoms to those that the disorder has already imposed. Whatever can be achieved in hospital is not enough, for the patient requires and deserves treatment that extends over a longer period of months or years. In addition, the patient needs rehabilitation that can only occur when he or she is living as a member of the general community, not separated from that community by bricks, stones, or glass. What this means is that the ultimate treatment of the schizophrenic patient will not be inpatient, but will be and should be ambulatory or outpatient, for it is out in the world, insofar as it is possible, that he or she should properly be. The better the patient can manage in the world that others inhabit, the more successful the treatment and management will have been. This point of view is not equivalent to that which says the patient must be kept out of the hospital at all costs, for there are of course times when the welfare and safety of both patient and others dictate that there be a period of treatment within a protective hospital environment. What must be clear is that truncating treatment at the time of discharge from the hospital is entirely inadequate to the needs of the patient and of other interested members of the community.

That part of the treatment of schizophrenia that takes place in the physician's office is linked to that which takes place elsewhere in the community: in the home, in the homes of relatives and friends, on the job, in clinics, and in agencies devoted to the care of patients with this chronic disorder. The coordination of all these efforts (medical, biochemical, psychological, and social) is of great importance. Numerous people have a role to play in these joint efforts. Some are professionals, as is the psychiatrist. Some are not, including members of the patient's family and those involved in lay organizations to help schizophrenic patients. Ideally, there will be some rational coordination of the efforts of the various individuals and groups. Without such coordination, the opportunity for the greatest possible help to the schizophrenic patient will be lost.

The Essential Focus of Treatment: The Individual Patient

The pursuit of understanding and knowledge about schizophrenia has been highly productive, particularly in recent decades. A great deal of important information has been garnered about genetic, biochemical, psychological, and social aspects of this disorder. The advantage of putting each of these areas under the highest power of our research microscopes, so to speak, is obvious, for in this way we have been able to add, one by one, building blocks to our understanding of a very complex problem. On the other hand, there is an undesirable side effect that can arise from the separation that is required for effective, reliable scientific scrutiny: in the process of dissecting the problem for purposes of research and teaching, we run the risk of losing sight of the essential object of our interest—the individual human being who is affected with schizophrenia. It is of course not the intention of academics to lose sight of the person, but throughout medicine in general it has been found that subspecialized interest and technological advances can easily lead to the loss of the primacy of the individual patient.

In a way, giving full attention to the individual means a return to something that was well recognized in the past, rather than creating something new. Many of the pioneer workers in psychotherapy or modified psychoanalysis understood well the unique importance of working with the individual patient (Chapter 4). John Whitehorn, then a psychiatrist at the McLean Hospital near Boston, was interested in the 1940s in the biochemical differences that he believed must exist in schizophrenic individuals. While drawing samples of blood for his investigations, he began to listen and talk to the patients and, although his training and interest until then had not been in psychotherapy, thought that what he heard had important meaning and relevance to the patients' illness. This led him, for the remainder of his career, to pursue efforts to understand the psychological characteristics of these patients, including efforts to help them through psychotherapeutic interventions (Whitehorn and Betz 1954, 1960).

The early workers who dealt intensively with schizophrenic patients recognized the merit of knowing the patient as an individual person. They did not have the advantage of information that has more recently become available about the genetic, biochemical, familial, and social aspects of schizophrenia. Having that advantage today, we must not then surrender the equally important advantage of appreciating the individual perceptions, feelings, and thoughts of the schizophrenic patient. There is still much to be gained from a comprehensive approach such as that taken by another pioneer in psychiatry, Adolf Meyer, who taught that we must pay equal attention to the biological (including the genetic), the psychological (focusing on the individual), and the social (including the family) (Meyer 1934).

As earlier chapters have indicated, we have, since the time of those early psychotherapists working with schizophrenic patients, learned that even though our central appreciation is of the point of view and experiences of the schizophrenic patient himself or herself, there are other ways of working with him or her that are equally valid and valuable. They include dealing with the patient as an organism with chemical problems (Chapters 7 and 8), as a member of a family (Chapters 3 and 6), as someone who has a disorder with which others also have to cope (Chapter 6), and as a member of a complex society where helpful forces can be mobilized in a variety of ways (Chapter 9). Although this chronic disorder needs to be addressed in long-term ways (Chapter 1), it will also require at times active intervention when critical situations arise (Chapter 10). Ideally there should be some coordination of these various efforts, but always with the central focus being the individual who is suffering from the disorder. A psychiatric approach that is broad and all-encompassing will add a great deal to the welfare of all concerned, but will not have its greatest effect if in the process the focus upon the individual is lost.

Essential Elements of Treatment: The Therapist and the Therapeutic Relationship

Some of what we have described in this book is objective enough to be prescribed at arm's length, and being that objective, can still be helpful. Computer programs could exist that could, being fed the necessary information, make the diagnosis of schizophrenia and prescribe appropriate medication to be taken by the patient. Associations could be organized to be of help to schizophrenic patients and their families by people who had never dealt with schizophrenic individuals. Money could be raised by legislators and social programs put into effect without the people involved ever having dealt personally with someone who suffers from schizophrenia. However, the same cannot be said for the direct treatment of schizophrenia.

If someone undertakes such treatment, he or she will discover that a very personal and emotional undertaking is at hand. Considerable research has indicated what essential elements are contributed by the psychotherapist. Much of this has been through controlled studies (Karasu 1982), and some has been through the observations of clinicians (Greben 1984). Probably the most impressive and certainly the most moving evidence of the central importance of the therapist has been provided in accounts written by former patients who have felt helped by the efforts of their former therapists. I will quote briefly from two examples.

Harry Guntrip, originally a minister, became a psychoanalyst with a strong interest in an object relations approach. He arranged to undergo psychoanalysis with two prominent British psychoanalysts: Ronald Fairbairn and Donald Winnicott. This gave him the opportunity to compare the contributions that each had made to the psychoanalytic work. Guntrip wrote the following late in his life (Guntrip 1975):

Conclusion: Essentials and Prospects for the Future

In the last resort good therapists are born not trained, and they make the best use of training. . . . I already held the view that psychoanalytic therapy is not a purely theoretical but a truly understanding personal relationship. . . . I went to [Fairbairn] because we stood philosophically on the same ground and no actual intellectual disagreements would interfere with the analysis. But the capacity for forming a relationship does not depend solely on our theory. Not everyone has the same facility for forming personal relationships, and we can all form a relationship more easily with some people than with others. The unpredictable factor of "natural fit" enters in. Thus, in spite of his conviction Fairbairn did not have the same capacity for natural, spontaneous "personal relating" that Winnicott had. . . . (pp. 145–146)

Psychoanalytic therapy is not like a "technique" of the experimental sciences, an objective "thing-in-itself" working automatically. It is a process of interaction, a function of two variables, the personalities of two people working together towards free spontaneous growth. The analyst grows as well as the analysand. There must be something wrong if an analyst is static when he deals with such dynamic experiences. For me, Fairbairn built as a person on what my father did for me, and as an analyst enabled me to discover in great detail how my battles for independence of mother from three and a half to seven years had grown into my personality make-up. Without that I could have deteriorated in old age into as awkward a person as my mother. Winnicott, a totally different type of personality, understood and filled the emptiness my mother left in the first three and a half years. I needed them both and had the supreme good fortune to find both. . . . (p. 155)

All through life we take into ourselves both good and bad figures who either strengthen or disturb us, and it is the same in psychoanalytic therapy: it is the meeting and interacting of two real people in all its complex possibilities. (p. 156)

I have quoted Guntrip for several reasons. First, his essay is remarkable in that a leading figure in psychoanalysis has so candidly, publicly recorded his personal experiences in treatment. Second, he makes so clearly the point that what happens in successful therapy is very much a function of who the therapist is and how he or she interacts with the patient. Third, even though it is psychoanalysis Guntrip is discussing, all of the same factors apply in not only the psychotherapy, but in the general psychiatric management of the schizophrenic patients we are discussing. Dealing with such patients, using the various therapeutic modalities that we have described in earlier chapters, involves the use of the therapist as a person, not a distant, entirely objective person, but a close-at-hand, sufficiently objective, yet subjectively involved real person.

The second author I wish to quote on the matter of the relevance of the therapist's personal qualities is Hannah Green. She was treated for a schizophrenic illness in adolescence by Frieda Fromm-Reichmann (see also Chapter 1). Some years later, Green was presented with the Frieda Fromm-Reichmann Award by the American Academy of Psychoanalysis for her contribution to the understanding of psychiatry and schizophrenia through her writing of *I Never Promised You a Rose Garden*. On that occasion, Green said (Green 1967, pp. 74–76):

> I wanted to speak in praise of my doctor who honors this award with her name. . . .
> We had one running difference of opinion on which neither of us ever gave ground. I have the last word now only by the crude expediency of having outlived her. She held that psychiatry was a science and I said it was an art. She believed that the gifts she had—humor, empathy, indignation, intuition, a first-rate intellect, linguistic sensitivity, and the endearing quality of not exploiting her patients to prove herself or her theories—she believed that these things could be taught and learned, and that anyone who was reasonably intelligent could cultivate them to a degree equal to or exceeding her own. I think she was wrong. . . . In spite of her talk about psychotherapy being a science, she had little of the professionalistic cant that puts any theory ahead of the patient. I believe she would swing from the chandelier like Tarzan if she thought it would help; and she knew the book well enough to throw it away, or at least not to read it while the patient was watching. It must be difficult not to exploit patients to prove a theory—I know it happens in your pro-

fession and in others—but Frieda never did it to me and I am grateful.

But there are things you can never know unless you have been on both sides of the bars. One is the tremendous distance between sickness and health, another is the incredible value of the work you do, and another is the gratitude that the recovered have for the facts of a normal contact with life. These are things beyond value and beyond description—so with my thanks for this award, I will now wake up to find myself stirring the soup and reading my sons' report cards, and you may find yourselves back home again, raising the dead.

Once again, I quote the words of someone whose views have relevance to our subject for several reasons. First, Green emphatically makes the point that her therapist succeeded to such an extent because of her innate qualities of character and because of her various talents. This is not to say that most practitioners can hope to have Fromm-Reichmann's skills as a therapist and as a teacher, but probably the most important lesson to derive from Green's views is that each of us needs to be true to his or her own values and gifts, and not be swayed to follow some generalized prescription of how a therapist should be.

Second, Green appropriately underscores the individuality of the therapist as well as the uniqueness of the therapeutic combination. One can presume that her therapist was not identical with all of her patients but reacted to them in ways that seemed to her most appropriate for their specific personalities, capacities, and needs.

Third, in her final comments, Green provides us with a valuable reminder of the distance between severe mental illness and a relatively normal mental and emotional state. Our schizophrenic patients know the terror and pain of such illness. Those whom we are able to help toward greater normalcy have much reason to be grateful, as have we, for having the opportunity to play a part in a change of such great importance. The human mind, body, and spirit can fall prey to many kinds of pain. Schizophrenia subjects the person to numerous varieties of pain that are as severe as any with which people can be afflicted. It is important to bear in mind that whatever technological advances become available for dealing with schizophrenia, the human factors, on the parts of both the patient and the therapist, will remain of essential importance.

Prospects for the Future

So much has been learned about schizophrenia in the past century that it seems reasonable to expect that the coming decades will bring improvements in many if not all of the areas that we have addressed in this book. In all likelihood, the most striking changes will occur in the more technical dimensions of prevention, management, and treatment.

Since our diagnostic tools, both biochemical and electronic, have improved so greatly in recent years, it is reasonable to expect, to begin with, that we will come to know much more about the genetic aspects of schizophrenia. This will be accompanied by a more complete knowledge of both the neurological and biochemical lesions of schizophrenic patients. At the same time, even more specific and efficacious medications will certainly be developed, perhaps including some that take directions entirely unanticipated by us at present.

Similarly, there may be improved social ways of coping with this widespread disorder. Certainly there have been improved facilities available in recent decades, as the economic and personal price paid by so many patients and families has become apparent. The social problems are of enormous magnitude, and neither the hospital nor the community approach has thus far been successful overall, although impressive pilot projects and programs have already taken place in a number of areas and in a number of countries.

Considerable educational strides have been made in recent years. Psychiatrists of various persuasions, both biological and psychodynamic, have addressed the great problem of this disorder, and on all sides the general public has been exposed to more information about schizophrenia. We are still far from a satisfactory situation, but a good beginning has been made, so that this most important mental and emotional illness is less denied, avoided, neglected, and hidden away than has ever been the case in the past. It would be falsely optimistic to suggest that serious prejudice and negative attitudes no longer attach to schizophrenia, for they still do. Nonetheless, in relative terms, there is increasingly a more open and rational approach to such matters, and it is to be hoped that we will see an increased attitude of open inquiry toward this problem, and a fuller application of scientific scrutiny to each of its various aspects.

In summary, our view is the following. In all likelihood, the methods and tools of science will continue to produce new knowledge about schizophrenia: its causes, its pathology, its social effects, its treatment, and, it is hoped, ultimately its prevention. That knowledge will surely continue to improve the lot of those who have this disorder, and those close to them who are so profoundly affected. It is also likely to improve the capacity of psychiatrists to be of help, and, as a result, to allow them to feel more competent in their approach to this problem. Meanwhile, even before such further knowledge becomes available to us, there is a great deal that can be done to help.

It is in a small minority of cases that we can appropriately speak of cure. This is no different from the situation that confronts medicine with so many disorders, in all specialties. At present a great deal can be done to ameliorate the distress of schizophrenic patients and those close to them. We have described the present state of the various tools that can be useful. It is important that these tools be understood separately, and especially well mastered by those with particular interest in one or more of them. It is equally important, as stated earlier, that there be some coordination of the use of these various tools, for in this way the ultimate total benefit will be considerably magnified.

In the comprehensive office treatment of schizophrenia, at the present state of our knowledge, much can be achieved in the way of improvement in the lives of patients and their families, and in the resulting benefit to society at large. We hope that psychiatrists will increasingly come to know the satisfaction that can come from working with patients with schizophrenia.

References

Greben SE: Love's Labor: Twenty-five Years of Experience in the Practice of Psychotherapy. New York, Schocken Books, 1984

Green H: "In praise of my doctor"—Frieda Fromm-Reichmann. Contemporary Psychoanalysis 4:73–77, 1967

Guntrip H: My experience of analysis with Fairbairn and Winnicott (How complete a result does psycho-analytic therapy achieve?). International Review of Psycho-Analysis 2:145–156, 1975

Karasu TB: Psychotherapy Research: Methodological and Efficacy Issues. Washington, DC, American Psychiatric Association, 1982

Meyer A: The psychobiological point of view, in The Problem of Mental Disorders. Edited by Bentley N, Cowdrey E. New York, McGraw-Hill, 1934

Whitehorn JC, Betz BA: A study of psychotherapeutic relationships between physicians and schizophrenic patients. Am J Psychiatry 111:321–331, 1954

Whitehorn JC, Betz BA: Further studies of the doctor as a crucial variable in the outcome of treatment of schizophrenic patients. Am J Psychiatry 117:215–223, 1960